Constitutional Change
in the United States

CONSTITUTIONAL CHANGE IN THE UNITED STATES

A Comparative Study of the Role of Constitutional Amendments, Judicial Interpretations, and Legislative and Executive Actions

John R. Vile

Westport, Connecticut
London

Library of Congress Cataloging-in-Publication Data

Vile, John R.
    Constitutional change in the United States : a comparative study
of the role of constitutional amendments, judicial interpretations,
and legislative and executive actions / John R. Vile.
        p.   cm.
    Includes bibliographical references and index.
    ISBN 0–275–94918–4 (alk. paper)
        1. United States—Constitutional law—Amendments.   I. Title.
    KF4557.V55   1994
    342.73´03—dc20
    [347.3022]   94–1140

British Library Cataloguing in Publication Data is available.

Library of Congress Catalog Card Number: 94–1140
ISBN: 0–275–94918–4

First published in 1994

Praeger Publishers, 88 Post Road West, Westport, CT 06881
An imprint of Greenwood Publishing Group, Inc.

Printed in the United States of America

The paper used in this book complies with the
Permanent Paper Standard issued by the National
Information Standards Organization (Z39.48–1984).

10 9 8 7 6 5 4 3 2

To Gary and Norma Freedom

Contents

Preface

Although I have now been writing and thinking about the constitutional amending process for fifteen years, probably no one would have been more surprised than me if someone were to have told me when I began my research that I would now be writing my sixth book related to the subject. The writer of Ecclesiastes 12:12 (AV) said that "of making many books there is no end," and my own explorations seem to confirm his observations, but, whatever overlaps there may be, I think that readers will see that each of my books, including this one, has explored a new facet of constitutional change.

I am particularly fascinated by the specific subject of this book because it appeals to two of my scholarly interests. As a researcher, I have devoted most of my attention to the formal constitutional amending process, but as a teacher I have now been instructing classes in American government and American constitutional law for more than sixteen years. It is fitting, then, that I am particularly fascinated by the interaction of these two processes, which, along with changes initiated by the legislative and executive branches, are the central focus of this book.

It has been my experience that however much progress can be made dealing with changes initiated through the amending process, ultimately all such studies begin and end with the observation that not all alterations have been initiated through this formal process. Similarly, there is growing recognition within the discipline of constitutional law itself that a complete account of American constitutional development requires attention to legislative and executive actions as well as to judicial decisions. While some texts now deal with this latter need, it is still possible to lose sight of the fact that it is a Constitution (and its amendments) that such actions and decisions are explaining.

This book is designed to show that American constitutional development has proceeded via at least three major constitutional highways and that (to continue the metaphor) each comes with its own points of scenic interest. Each road has its own advantages and disadvantages, and none is likely to take the place of the other two. The belief that constitutional amendments should neither be studied in isolation nor forgotten is thus the motivating thesis behind this work.

Like all scholars, my debts are far too numerous for me to list them all. I continue to enjoy the comfort of a loving family and supportive friends for whom I am grateful. I continue to receive extraordinary good service from Betty McFall, the MTSU interlibrary loan librarian and others who work there, especially John Marshall who recently retired from the reference desk. My students and colleagues continue to stimulate my academic development, and Middle Tennessee State University continues to lend its support to my efforts—a grant for summer research was especially helpful in getting this particular book started, and support from my dean, John McDaniel, helped see it to completion. I owe special thanks to a gifted and congenial brother-in-law, Paul Christensen, for helping me with the graphics in this book. I would also like to thank James Dunton, Richard Sillett, and Jeanne Lesinski at Praeger for their valuable assistance.

I dedicate this book to two friends, one of whom was a colleague in the Department of Social Sciences at McNeese State University in Lake Charles, Louisiana and both of whom my family and I were fortunate enough to have as neighbors during our stay there. Their friendship, good humor, hospitality, and phone calls continue to mean much to us.

Constitutional Change in the United States

Chapter 1

The Process of Constitutional Amendment and Constitutional Change

While most contemporary Americans undoubtedly take the power for granted, the inclusion of a formal amending process marked the United States Constitution as fairly unique when it was written and ratified.[1] Article V of the U.S. Constitution outlines the process of amendment, a process requiring two steps, proposal and ratification.[2] It takes a two-thirds vote of both Houses of Congress or a special constitutional convention called by Congress at the request of two-thirds of the state legislatures to propose amendments. To become part of the Constitution, three-fourths of the states must in turn ratify these proposals; Congress specifies whether the states will do this through their legislatures or through special ratifying conventions.[3] The amending process is thus a difficult one[4] which requires supermajorities and reflects the federal nature of the U.S. Constitution.[5] The only currently applicable stated limit on the amending process providing that states shall not be deprived of their equal representation in the Senate without their consent reflects this federal dimension.

THE DESIGN AND PURPOSE OF ARTICLE V

Having participated in a revolution that was precipitated when the British ignored colonial petitions for reform and redress, the Founders clearly viewed the constitutional amending process as an alternative to violent change. The scholarly George Mason of Virginia accordingly argued at the Constitutional Convention that it was better to provide for constitutional changes "in an easy, regular and Constitutional way than to trust to chance and violence."[6] Subsequently, the safety-valve analogy became commonplace in the writings on constitutional amendments.[7] Thoughtful Americans understood that a Constitution with a formal amending process to serve as such a safety-valve was less likely to explode into revolutionary violence than one without such a process.

While proponents of the U.S. Constitution claimed that the amending process guarded "equally against that extreme facility, which would render the Constitution too mutable; and that extreme difficulty, which might perpetuate its discovered faults,"[8] the nation has adopted only twenty-seven amendments, and ten of these were so contemporaneous with the writing of the document and so much the result of the debate over constitutional ratification that they are usually considered part of the original document itself.[9] The nation has adopted a number of other amendments, most notably the Thirteenth through Fifteenth,[10] and the Sixteenth through Nineteenth[11] in clusters. Thus, the written Constitution has remained relatively unchanged throughout much of its history.[12]

THE LANGUAGE OF CONSTITUTIONALISM

The difficulty of adopting amendments[13] and the paucity of amendments that have been added to the national Constitution[14] have undoubtedly contributed to the development of other means of peaceful constitutional adaptation.[15] Unfortunately, the language of constitutionalism is not uniform and does not always lead to clear thinking on the subject. As Thomas Grey has stated, constitutionalism is "one of those concepts, evocative and persuasive in its connotations yet cloudy in its analytic and descriptive content, which at once enrich and confuse political discourse."[16] It is nonetheless important to attain as great clarity on the subject as is possible.

One dichotomy which applies to a nation like the United States is the distinction between its (uppercase) "Constitution" and its (lowercase) "constitution."[17] Charles Miller describes the former as the "formal written document describing a pattern of legal rules and institutions that function for political purposes" and the latter as "the pattern of political relationships which may be, but need not be, defined in legal instruments."[18] While he does not use the capital and lowercase *c* to distinguish them, David M. Walker notes that a constitution may be either "the body of rules prescribing the major elements of the structure and organization of any group of persons," or "the fundamental political and legal structure of government of a distinct political community, settling such matters as the head of state, the legislature, executive and judiciary, their composition, powers and relations."[19] Walker further indicates that "every state has a constitution [in the second sense], since every state functions on the basis of certain fundamental principles and rules."[20]

Walker proceeds to mention yet another distinction, that between "written" and "unwritten" constitutions.[21] Since so-called unwritten constitutions are also embodied in part in written laws and agreements, other scholars have suggested that the hallmark of so-called written constitutions is not so much that they are written as that their language cannot be changed by ordinary legislative means.[22] Thus, it was especially common earlier in this century to follow James Bryce and distinguish between so-called flexible and rigid constitutions,[23] with Constitutions once designated as "written" now being classified as "rigid" and those which were "unwritten" now being designated as "flexible."[24]

Whatever description he or she ultimately chooses, the student of American politics must cope with the fact that the capital C, written, rigid Constitution, even as amended, gives an incomplete description of the workings of government, even regarding some relatively important matters which clearly have a "constitutional" dimension.[25] While political scientists in Great Britain are much more likely than Americans to speak of customs and usages or refer to the "unwritten constitution,"[26] neither concept is unique to a parliamentary system.[27]

Thus, it is difficult, if not impossible, to describe the workings of American politics without serious attention to political parties, but neither are parties mentioned in the Document of 1787, nor have they been described in any subsequent amendment.[28] While the rise of political parties may be considered extra capital C Constitutional from start to finish, other developments more clearly falling within the admittedly elusive "constitutional" category share in never having been reflected in Constitutional amendments. The only indication of the Revolution of 1800 (the terminology is itself suggestive of the elusive relationship between peaceful change and that which is not)[29] by which the Jeffersonian Republicans repudiated Federalist constitutional theory[30] and took the reins of power is the aforementioned Twelfth Amendment. Judicial review, today considered absolutely essential to the whole idea of checks and balances and of constitutional government, may be implied, but it is certainly not stated in the Constitution itself.[31] The Constitution gives no record of the Louisiana Purchase of 1803 or the Embargo of 1808, both of which required expansive interpretations of federal power and the first of which Jefferson himself thought should not be consummated without a Constitutional amendment.[32] There is no archaeological relic,[33] no ring on the Constitutional tree,[34] indicating the emotions that were stirred, the issues aired, or the constitutional crises precipitated by the Tariff Crisis of 1828–32. One could never guess simply by reading the Constitution and its amendments that questions of substantive due process in economic interpretation were major topics of constitutional dimensions for decades.[35] Not only is there no direct evidence in the Constitution of the revolution initiated by the U.S. Supreme Court's "switch in time that saved nine" in 1937, but the Constitution is similarly silent about the changes wrought by Lyndon Johnson's Great Society, the "incorporation" of nearly all of the guarantees of the Bill of Rights into the Due Process Clause of the Fourteenth Amendment, or of the so-called Reagan Revolution,[36] all of which have significantly affected understandings of federalism and of the role of government in society. Amendments have clearly constituted but a subset of constitutional change in America.

ADDITIONAL CONSIDERATIONS

Two additional factors complicate a discussion of American constitutionalism. First is the fact that, while the judicial branch has special responsibility for both (capital *C*) Constitutional and (lowercase *c*) constitutional issues, other branches of government (either on their own or in conjunction with the courts) also contribute to and modify these constitutional understandings.[37] In the words of two commentators, "The process is not linear, with the courts issuing the final word. The process is circular, turning back on itself again and again until society is satisfied with the outcome."[38] Similarly, another scholar argues that a virtue of mechanisms for judicial deference is that "they implicitly or explicitly share responsibility for giving meaning to the Constitution."[39] Thus, just as focus on the formal constitutional amending process does not fully describe the constitutional changes which take place in the United States, traditional treatments of "constitutional law" which focus almost exclusively on the role of the federal courts, and the U.S. Supreme Court in particular, may also not fully capture the forces of change that are at work.[40]

Further complicating the situation is that some scholars have convincingly argued that the formal written Constitution can itself change in meaning through "authoritative interpretations."[41] These scholars contend that even the words of the written Constitution must be understood in the context of "the interaction over time of framers, judges, legislatures, and executive officials."[42]

DIAGRAMMING THE PROCESSES OF
CONSTITUTIONAL CHANGE

In short, over time formal amendments may change the written Constitution just as interpretations and practices may alter its contemporary meaning. Moreover, important developments within the wider "constitution" may influence and even determine interpretations of the Constitution and/or dramatically affect governmental operations without ever being incorporated into the document.

The relationship between change instituted by constitutional amendments and other forms of governmental changes which do not require such amendments is diagrammed in Figure 1.1, with the ambiguity of deciding which issues are properly "constitutional" being symbolized by the use of a broken line.[43]

THREE SOURCES OF CONSTITUTIONAL
CHANGE IN AMERICA

The thesis of this book is that there are three primary mechanisms and sets of players that initiate constitutional change in the United States. There is, of course, the process of Constitutional amendment outlined in this chapter. Thousands of proposed changes and twenty-seven formal amendments stand witness to the power of this mechanism.[44]

While amendments are the only way that changes can be formally incorporated into the language of the written Constitution, judicial interpre-

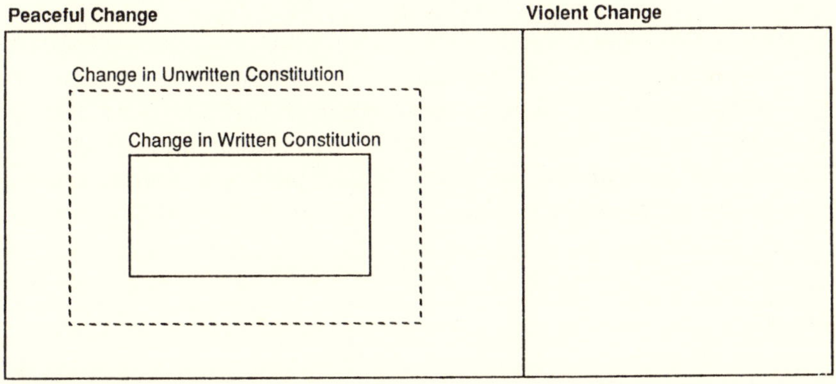

Peaceful Change   Violent Change

Change in Unwritten Constitution

Change in Written Constitution

Figure 1.1
Governmental Change

tations serve to expand and clarify interpretations of that document as well as to initiate and signal changes in the nation's more embracive (lowercase *c*) constitution. Given the judiciary's long-standing claim "to say what the law is,"[45] there is wisdom in Woodrow Wilson's observation that the Supreme Court constitutes "a kind of Constitutional Convention in continuous session"[46] and in Mason and Stevenson's claim that "one could memorize the written document word for word," but that, without knowledge of the judicial gloss on the Constitution, "still know little or nothing of its meaning."[47]

Scholars increasingly recognize that the judiciary is not the sole expositor of the written Constitution, and the courts certainly have no monopoly over influencing and interpreting the nation's lowercase *c* constitution. Consistent with the representative character of American government and the Constitution's emphasis on elections, although theirs may not always be the final word, the elected branches are responsible for initiating many such changes. These branches initiate such changes via presidential orders and directives as well as congressional legislation.[48]

THE PURPOSE OF THIS BOOK

Except perhaps in introductory American government textbooks, discussions of lawmaking, of judicial review, and of constitutional amendment generally proceed independently, and each is certainly complicated enough to be so treated. In treating these processes in that fashion, however, the elusive relationships among these processes, and their overall impact on change, may be slighted. Accordingly, in the pages that follow this author will examine each of these mechanisms as an engine of constitutional change, compare their relative merits and demerits, examine how these findings bear on existing theories of constitutional change, and ascertain what, if any, implications these findings have on the adequacy of the current formal process of constitutional amendment and the desirability of pursuing changes through this or through alternate routes.

NOTES

1. The origins of this process are discussed in John R. Vile, *Contemporary Questions Surrounding the Constitutional Amending Process* (Westport, CT: Praeger, 1993), pp. 1–2.

2. Article V reads as follows: "The Congress, whenever two thirds of both Houses shall deem it necessary, shall propose amendments to this Constitution, or, on the application of the legislatures of two thirds of the several States, shall call a convention for proposing amendments, which, in either case, shall be valid to all intents and purposes, as part of this Constitution, when ratified by the legislatures of three fourths of the several States, or by conventions in three fourths thereof, as the one or the other mode of ratification may be proposed by the Congress; Provided that no amendment which may be made prior to the year one thousand eight hundred and eight shall in any manner affect the first and fourth clauses in the ninth section of the first article; and that no State, without its consent, shall be deprived of its equal suffrage in the Senate."

A recent book chronicles the history of amendments in America and gives some overview of amendment controversies. See Richard B. Bernstein with Jerome Agel, *Amending America: If We Love the Constitution So Much, Why Do We Keep Trying to Change It?* (New York: Times Books, 1993). For an earlier account, see Alan P. Grimes, *Democracy and the Amendments to the Constitution* (Lexington, MA: Lexington Books, 1978). For a recent book which focuses less on the history of the amending process than on the solution to unresolved questions of procedure surrounding the amending process and the unused convention procedures, see Vile, *Contemporary Questions Surrounding the Constitutional Amending Process*. Also see Russell L. Caplan, *Constitutional Brinkmanship: Amending the Constitution by National Convention* (New York: Oxford University Press, 1988).

3. The only amendment to be ratified by convention to date was the Twenty-First. See Everett S. Brown, "The Ratification of the Twenty-First Amendment," *The American Political Science Review* 29 (December 1935), pp. 1005–17. Also see *Ratification of the Twenty-first Amendment to the Constitution of the United States*, Department of State Publication No. 573 (Washington: United States Government Printing Office, 1934).

In other nations, popular referenda are sometimes used to ratify constitutional amendments. See Jorge Manrazo, "La Reforma Constitucional. Un Estudio Comparativo Con Enfasis Al Caso Mexicano Y NorteAmericano," *Derecho constitucional comparado Mexico-Estados Unidos*, ed. James Smith, (Mexico: Universidad Nacional Autonoma de Mexico, 1990), pp. 193–200. Some have suggested that such referenda or the alternative convention mechanism would be more democratic. See William H. Pedrick and Richard C. Dahl, "Let the People Vote! Ratification of Constitutional Amendments by Convention," *Arizona Law Review* 30 (1988), pp. 243–56.

4. Mary F. Berry, "How Hard It Is To Change," *New York Times Magazine* (September 13, 1987), pp. 93–98.

5. Ruth Bader Ginsberg, President Clinton's first appointment to the U.S. Supreme Court, has thus noted that "This two step [amending] process, requiring supermajorities at both proposal and ratification stages, promotes cautious deliberation and demands a strong consensus before constitutional change is ordered."

See "On Amending the Constitution: A Plea for Patience," *University of Arkansas at Little Rock Law Journal* 12 (1989–90), p. 681.

6. Quoted in Max Farrand, ed., *The Records of the Federal Convention of 1787*, vol. 2 (New Haven, CT: Yale University Press, 1966), p. 202.

7. See Joseph Story, *Commentaries on the Constitution of the United States*, vol. 3 (Boston: Hillard, Gray and Company, 1833), pp. 686–87. Also see George Williams, "What If Any, Limitations Are There Upon the Power To Amend the Constitution of the United States," *Virginia Law Register* n.s. 6 (July 1920), p. 167.

The safety-valve analogy was consistent with various other mechanical analogies that were used, especially in the nineteenth century, to understand the Constitution. On this point, see Michael Kammen, *A Machine That Would Go of Itself: The Constitution in American Culture* (New York: Alfred A. Knopf, 1987). Woodrow Wilson and others who have followed have sought to understand the Constitution through use of more evolutionary analogies. For a discussion of this change, see John R. Vile, *The Constitutional Amending Process in American Political Thought* (New York: Praeger, 1992), pp. 139–40.

8. James Madison in *Federalist* No. 43. Alexander Hamilton, James Madison, and John Jay, *The Federalist Papers*, intro. by Clinton Rossiter (New York: New American Library, 1961), p. 278.

9. See comments of Justice Miller in the *Slaughterhouse Cases*, 16 Wallace 36, 67 (1873).

10. These amendments—which will be discussed in greater detail in the next chapter—respectively outlawed involuntary servitude, defined citizenship rights applicable to all persons "born or naturalized in the United States," and guaranteed that voting rights would not be "denied or abridged . . . on account of race, color, or previous condition of servitude." They were ratified between 1865 and 1870. Grimes refers to these as "The Northern Amendments." See his *Democracy and the Amendments*, pp. 31–64.

For a recent reinterpretation of these amendments which argues that they should be interpreted broadly in light of the aims of their abolitionist proponents, see David A. J. Richards, *Conscience and the Constitution: History, Theory and Law of the Reconstruction Amendments* (Princeton, NJ: Princeton University Press, 1993). For an earlier contrasting view, see Raoul Berger, *Government by Judiciary: The Transformation of the Fourteenth Amendment* (Cambridge, MA: Harvard University Press, 1977).

11. These amendments—which will be also be discussed in greater detail in the next chapter—respectively legalized the national income tax, provided for direct election of U.S. Senators, mandated alcoholic prohibition, and extended the suffrage to women. They were ratified from 1913 to 1920. Grimes calls these "The Western Amendments" because of their origin in the Western states where tides of populism and progressivism, which contributed to these amendments, were particularly powerful. See Grimes, *Democracy and the Amendments*, pp. 65–100.

12. Grimes notes that there have been five periods during which two or more amendments have been added to the Constitution and one instance of a single amendment (the Twenty-Second). He further notes that, "The average time elapsed between eras of amendments has been about twenty-nine years." See Ibid., pp. 157–58.

The Twenty-Seventh Amendment, ratified in 1992 since the publication of Grimes's book, might constitute another instance of a single amendment, since the previous amendment had been ratified twenty-one years before in 1971. Alternatively, the amendment, originally proposed as part of the Bill of Rights, could be linked to this original cluster of amendments. For discussion of the Twenty-Seventh Amendment, see Richard B. Bernstein, "The Sleeper Wakes: The History and Legacy of the Twenty-Seventh Amendment," *Fordham Law Review* 61 (December 1992), pp. 497–557.

13. There has been periodic criticism in American history that the amending process was too difficult, particularly in the period that marked the U.S. Civil War and the period Progressive Era. Some of these critiques are described in Vile, *The Constitutional Amending Process in American Political Thought*, pp. 95–105, 137–50. The most cogent recent argument suggesting that the U.S. amending process may be too difficult is made by Donald S. Lutz, "Toward a Theory of Constitutional Amendment," paper presented at the American Political Science Association in Chicago, Illinois, September 1992, p. 33. In a survey of thirty constitutions, Lutz found that the only one with a more difficult procedure for constitutional amendments than that in the United States was Yugoslavia, which, in light of recent developments in that nation, can hardly be viewed as a favorable comparison.

14. While constitutional change at the national level has proceeded quite slowly, states have radically different traditions, coming much closer to Jefferson's vision that constitutions should be changed every generation. For Jefferson's views, see Vile, *The Constitutional Amending Process in American Political Thought*, pp. 63–67. For discussion of the state tradition of constitutional change, see Morton Keller, "The Politics of State Constitutional Revision, 1820–1930," in *The Constitutional Convention as an Amending Device*, ed. Kermit L. Hall, Harold M. Hyman, and Leon V. Sigal (Washington, DC: The American Historical Association and The American Political Science Association, 1981).

15. It is fascinating, however, that no full-scale revision has been made in the Constitution since 1787. For a survey of such proposals, see John R. Vile, *Rewriting the United States Constitution: An Examination of Proposals from Reconstruction to the Present* (New York: Praeger, 1991). Also see Steven R. Boyd, *Alternative Constitutions for the United States: A Documentary History* (Westport, CT: Greenwood Press, 1992). For a well-argued critique of recurring proposals to revamp American government along the lines of a parliamentary system, see Thomas O. Sargentich, "The Limits of the Parliamentary Critique of the Separation of Powers," *William and Mary Law Review* 34 (Spring 1993), pp. 679–739.

16. "Constitutionalism: An Analytic Framework," in *Constitutionalism*, ed. J. Roland Pennock and John W. Chapman (New York: New York University Press, 1979), p. 189.

17. For further reflections on the distinction between a (capital *C*) Constitution and a (lowercase *c*) constitution, see William F. Harris II, *The Interpretable Constitution* (Baltimore, MD: Johns Hopkins University Press, 1993). Also see Walter F. Murphy, James E. Fleming, and William F. Harris, eds., *American Constitutional Interpretation* (Mineola, NY: Foundation Press, 1986).

18. Charles A. Miller, *The Supreme Court and the Uses of History* (Cambridge, MA: Harvard University Press, Belknap Press, 1969), p. 150.

19. See *The Oxford Companion to Law* (Oxford: Clarendon Press, 1980), p. 277.

20. Ibid.

21. Ibid.

22. Herbert W. Horwill, *The Usages of the American Constitution* (Port Washington, NY: Kennikat Press, 1969 reprint of 1925), p. 9. For further discussions of such differences, see John R. Vile, "Three Kinds of Constitutional Founding and Change: The Convention Model and Its Alternatives," *Political Science Quarterly* (December 1993).

23. James Bryce, "Flexible and Rigid Constitutions," *Constitutions* (Germany: Scientia Verlag Aalen, 1980; reprint of New York and London, 1905).

24. For discussion of these classifications which corresponded to a time of intense criticism of the formal Article V amending process in America, see chapter 8 of Vile, *The Constitutional Amending Process in American Political Thought*.

Carl J. Friedrich, *Constitutional Government and Democracy* (Boston: Ginn and Company, 1946), p. 139, shares this author's concern that the term *rigid* appears to be pejorative; Friedrich suggested that *firm* would be a better designation for such constitutions.

25. James W. Ceasar has noted the way that constitutional systems are influenced by the political cultures. "Modern behavioral political science has joined traditional political science in extending the study of regimes beyond their formal mechanisms to such other factors as informal structures (e.g., parties and interest groups), social structure (e.g., class and ethnic composition), and political culture (e.g., animating beliefs and ways of thinking about the political world). It is to these other factors, no less than to the formal mechanisms, that we must look to understand how any system works." See *Liberal Democracy and Political Science* (Baltimore, MD: Johns Hopkins University Press, 1990), p. 180. M.J.C. Vile has, however, pointed out that this does not therefore negate the importance of "constitutions." See his *Constitutionalism and the Separation of Powers* (Oxford: Clarendon Press, 1967), p. 312.

26. For a recent treatment of this subject published in England, see Michael Foley, *The Silence of Constitutions: Gaps, Abeyances and Political Temperament in the Maintenance of Government* (London: Routledge, 1989).

27. See Christopher Tiedeman, *The Unwritten Constitution of the United States* (New York: G. P. Putnam's Sons, 1890); Horwill, *The Usages of the Amer-*

ican Constitution; and Don K. Price, *America's Unwritten Constitution: Science, Religion, and Political Responsibility* (Cambridge, MA: Harvard University Press, 1985). In writing about America's unwritten constitution, Price, p. 9, notes that "the party conventions and the primary system, congressional committees and their staffs, the statutory structure of the executive departments, the Executive Office of the President, the press conference and television coverage, and freedom of information—none of these was established by the Constitution or foreseen by its framers, and all could be abolished without formal amendment."

Much of the recent literature involving the "unwritten constitution" in the United States has centered on the role of the Supreme Court in interpreting and enforcing such unwritten rules. See, for example, Suzanna Sherry, "The Founders' Unwritten Constitution," *The University of Chicago Law Review* 54 (1987), pp. 1127–77 and Thomas C. Grey, "Do We Have an Unwritten Constitution?" *Stanford Law Review* 27 (February 1975), pp. 703–18.

28. The Twelfth Amendment does serve as a kind of constitutional "marker" in that it was ratified largely to remedy a problem precipitated by the development of political parties and the party ticket for president and vice president, but the amendment is silent as to its own cause. See Richard B. Bernstein, "Fixing the Electoral College," *Constitution* 5 (Winter 1993), pp. 42–50.

29. Originally the term *revolution*—borrowed from astronomy—suggested "an orderly and legal procedure." The term apparently became associated with more violent tactics in the aftermath of the French Revolution. See Garry Wills, *Inventing America: Jefferson's Declaration of Independence* (Garden City, NY: Doubleday, 1978), pp. 51–52.

30. Arguably there was a much greater change in theory than in actual practice as Henry Adams's study of the Jefferson administration shows. See *The Formative Years: A History of the United States During the Administration of Jefferson and Madison*, vol. 1, ed. Herbert Agar (London: Collins, 1948), pp. 178–86.

31. Gerhard Casper, "Constitutionalism," *Encyclopedia of the American Constitution*, vol. 2, ed. Leonard W. Levy (New York: Macmillan, 1986), p. 479.

32. For relevant documents, see John R. Vile, *The Theory and Practice of Constitutional Change in America* (New York: Peter Lang, 1993), pp. 178–81.

33. The term is borrowed from Thomas E. Brennan, "Return to Philadelphia," *Cooley Law Review* 1 (1982), p. 20.

34. This particular analogy was suggested to this author by two metaphors used by William Van Alstyne, one of a "petrified" Constitution and a second of amendments serving the role of "cambrian rings" which are, like such geological evidences, "its best evidence of life and continuing growth," which "mark and record visible progress." See "Notes on a Bicentennial Constitution: Part I, Processes of Change," *University of Illinois Law Review* (1984), p. 956.

35. Indeed, it is difficult for us even to conceptualize the issues as contemporaries did. For a brilliant interpretation of this time period, see Howard Gillman, *The Constitution Besieged: The Rise and Demise of Lochner Era Police Powers Jurisprudence* (Durham, NC: Duke University Press, 1993). Also useful is Paul

Kens, *Judicial Power and Reform Politics: The Anatomy of Lochner v. New York* (Lawrence: University of Kansas Press, 1990).

36. References in the preceding discussion to the election of Presidents Jefferson and Reagan indicate that many changes in constitutional understandings in the United States occur through regular elections and, particularly, through "critical" or "realigning" elections. The election of Jefferson, although not of Reagan, is usually interpreted as an example of such an election. For the classic work on critical elections, see Walter D. Burnham, *Critical Elections and the Mainsprings of American Politics* (New York: W. W. Norton, 1970).

37. Among treatments which point to the important role that other governmental branches share in interpreting the U.S. Constitution, see Louis Fisher, *Constitutional Dialogues: Interpretation as Political Process* (Princeton, NJ: Princeton University Press, 1988); Cass R. Sunstein, *The Partial Constitution* (Cambridge, MA: Harvard University Press, 1993); and Robert A. Burt, *The Constitution in Conflict* (Cambridge, MA: Harvard University Press, 1992).

38. Louis Fisher and Neal Devins, *Political Dynamics of Constitutional Law* (St. Paul, MN: West Publishing, 1992), p. 10.

39. Robert F. Nagel, *Constitutional Cultures* (Berkeley: University of California Press, 1989), p. 25.

40. This may turn out to be one of the most important and enduring lessons to be gleaned from Bruce Ackerman's *We the People: Foundations* (Cambridge, MA: Harvard University Press, Belknap Press, 1991). Also see Neal S. Devins, "Correspondence: The Stuff of Constitutional Law," *Iowa Law Review* 77 (July 1992), pp. 1795–1801.

41. Stephen R. Munzer and James W. Nickel, "Does the Constitution Mean What It Always Meant?" *Columbia Law Review* 77 (November 1977), p. 1043.

42. Ibid., p. 1042.

43. The author is not sure that the dimensions of this figure are at all proportioned according to how frequently changes of various sorts actually do take place or according to how they should. Given that threats of violence may sometimes prove to be as effective as force itself, it is also possible that the line between peaceful and violent change should be symbolized by a broken rather than a solid line.

44. Akil Reed Amar has argued that amendments can be adopted outside the specified Article V framework through referenda. See "Philadelphia Revisited: Amending the Constitution Outside Article V," *University of Chicago Law Review* 55 (Fall 1988), pp. 1043–104. The weaknesses of this approach were treated in my *Contemporary Questions*, pp. 97–125 and are hence not repeated here.

45. Quotation is from Marshall's opinion in *Marbury v. Madison*, 1 Cranch (5 U.S.) 137, 177 (1803).

46. Quoted in Corwin, *The Constitution and What It Means Today*, 14th ed., revised by Harold W. Chase and Craig R. Ducat (Princeton, NJ: Princeton University Press, 1978), p. 5.

47. Alpheus T. Mason and Donald G. Stephenson, Jr., *American Constitutional Law*, 10th ed. (Englewood Cliffs, NJ: Prentice-Hall, 1993), p. 38.

48. To the three types of initiating change described here, Donald S. Lutz adds another, namely, "periodic replacement of the entire document." See "Toward a Theory of Constitutional Amendment," p. 1. I have chosen to treat such changes under the rubric of constitutional amendments both because the amending process in the United States provides for a constitutional convention and because, at the national level at least, this form of change is still a category of one from which generalizations are difficult.

Chapter 2

A Survey of Constitutional Amendments and Their Impact on Change

Just as one can distinguish between changes in a nation's written Constitution and its wider unwritten constitution, so too one can classify alterations in governments and Constitutions according to their relation to the status quo. This chapter examines this topic from the perspective of constitutional amendments. The next chapter will analyze changes which judicial review has initiated while the chapter that follows it will focus on changes initiated by executive orders and legislation.

TYPES OF CHANGES AMENDMENTS HAVE INITIATED

The idea of progress is an inextricable part of modern Western civilization,[1] and the Darwinian theory of evolution furthered this idea in the last two centuries.[2] Accordingly, when most Americans think of constitutional amendment, they probably think of progressive advancement. Similarly, historians of the amending process, like historians of the American republic itself, often describe amendments as a continual movement toward the progressive realization of a central goal or principle.[3] Before proceeding to affirm his belief that the proper denotation of amendment was simply "alteration or change," a legal writer earlier in this century thus noted that " 'amendment' contains in it an element of euphemism, of conceit in the proposer, an assumption that the proposal is an improvement."[4] Reflection would certainly confirm, however, that it is easier to ascertain the direction many nations take retrospectively rather than prospectively and that there is no inexorable law which guarantees that all changes represent improvement.

Rather than assume that all changes which amendments initiate are or must be progressive, this writer has decided to classify amendments not according to whether they have inaugurated good or bad, progressive or regressive, changes but rather according to the effect they have had on the status quo. Figure 2.1 should be suggestive.

Perhaps the most unlikely possibility in Figure 2.1 is that the nation might adopt an amendment simply to preserve the status quo, but one can certainly imagine scenarios where the amending process might be so used. This is because of the distinction drawn in the previous chapter between uppercase Constitutional change and lowercase constitutional change. If all aspects of government were delineated in a nation's written Constitution, then it would indeed be silly to list them there again.[5] Since the processes of government are broader than those outlined in the written Constitution, however, there may be occasions where it is desirable to preserve the status quo by officially incorporating the status quo into the written Constitution. Thus, those who fear that the current Supreme Court might reverse existing rights of women to obtain abortions (a concern undoubtedly more prominent in the Bush than in the Clinton administration) could rationally seek an amendment incorporating the current understanding into the Constitution.[6] Clearly, the line between preserving the status quo and forestalling changes is a fine one, but one can imagine an amendment serving as a preemptive strike, attempting once and forever to preserve the status quo against foes real and imagined.

Because nations rarely move inexorably in a single direction, amendments may also be adopted to reverse course. Indeed, biblical writers used the term *amend*, as in "amend your ways,"[7] to suggest a personal or societal return to earlier standards of behavior. As the discussion below will indicate, there is an example from American history of an amendment which

Constitutional amendments can:

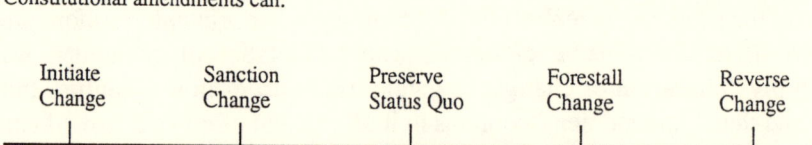

| Initiate Change | Sanction Change | Preserve Status Quo | Forestall Change | Reverse Change |

Figure 2.1
Constitutional Amendments and Change

was adopted to reverse another,[8] but the story is far more complicated than this isolated example might suggest. Again, the key to understanding is the recognition that the formal Constitution does not exclusively determine governmental behavior. It is thus possible that the people will adopt an amendment in order to return to an earlier pattern of governmental behavior that was understood and/or widely accepted but unwritten.[9]

Generally, however, amendments sanction or initiate change. The use of amendments to sanction change can again best be understood in light of the fact that changes in governmental practices and policies may be initiated outside the formal amending framework. When this happens, the nation may choose, for whatever reason, to give increased sanction and/or security to these changes by recognizing them in formal amendments.

Finally, amendments may indeed serve the function most typically associated with them, namely, initiating changes that lead in new directions. Similarly, amendments may apply long-standing principles to areas or groups not previously covered. Thus, the idea of extending voting rights was hardly new in 1971, but a constitutional amendment had not previously extended this right to individuals from eighteen to twenty-one years of age.

Here the limitations of figure 2.1 become evident. Much as proponents of rival ideological extremes sometimes converge, so too the line between amendments designed to initiate change and those designed to reverse change is a very fine one. Twenty years after *Roe v. Wade* (1973),[10] a "right to life amendment" could be viewed as either initiating a change in current practices and legal understandings or as returning to an earlier era. Thus, like some theories of change themselves, the best way to visualize change may be to think of a circle rather than a line.

CLASSIFYING AMENDMENTS IN AMERICA

Fortunately, scholars can approach the amending process not only theoretically but also historically. Accordingly, this chapter will examine each of the national amendments that has been proposed by the requisite majorities in Congress with a view toward analyzing which of the aforementioned uses of the amending process have been most prominent and what the relationships among these uses appear to be.

A Special Case: The New Constitution

Before looking at the amendments adopted under the authority of Article V, it is best to begin with the ratification of the Constitution itself.

Since many readers of this book are already familiar with the story of the Constitution's formation,[11] the narrative here will be merely a sketch.

A special convention held in Philadelphia and originally called by a group of delegates at the Annapolis Convention and subsequently confirmed by Congress wrote the current U.S. Constitution in the summer of 1787. A total of fifty-five delegates from all the thirteen states except Rhode Island attended. Although originally convened for the purpose of "revising the Articles of Confederation,"[12] the Virginia Plan influenced the delegates to consider a new form of government. Whereas the Articles had a single branch of government, the Virginia Plan proposed and the convention subsequently adopted a government of three branches. Although Congress under the Articles was unicameral and each state was represented equally, the Virginia Plan proposed and the Constitutional Convention subsequently adopted a bicameral Congress where states were represented in the lower house according to population. Whereas political scientists today classify the Articles as confederal, with primary power resting with the states, the new government was federal, with powers more evenly balanced between the states and the strengthened national government.[13] There were, in short, a host of differences between the old government and the new.

The differences between the two governments were apparent in Articles V and VII of the new Constitution. Whereas amendments under the Articles required proposal by Congress and subsequent ratification of all *thirteen* of the *state legislatures*,[14] Article VII of the new Constitution provided that it would go into effect when ratified by *conventions* in *nine* of the states. Moreover, under the terms of Article V of the new Constitution, while the majorities in Congress for proposing amendments were increased, amendments would become effective when ratified by only three-fourths rather than by all of the states. Clearly, the delegates to the Constitutional Convention chose to ignore, and in some cases to violate, the provisions of the Constitution they were replacing.[15]

The new Constitution did not, of course, start completely *de novo*, and so it is rather difficult to classify the document in a single one of the categories of change developed for this book. Significantly, however, Madison himself felt it necessary in *Federalist* No. 40 to defend the new creation against charges that it was unauthorized, and among his arguments was that the Framers thought it was important that "the means should be sacrificed to the end, rather than the end to the means."[16] Madison explained that "the great principles of the Constitution proposed by the convention may be considered less as absolutely new than as the expression of principles which are found in the Articles of Confederation,"[17] but, in the end, Madison argued that even if the members of the Convention had exceeded their powers, the Constitution should ultimately be judged on its own merits.[18]

THE BILL OF RIGHTS

The first amendments added to the U.S. Constitution were those found in the Bill of Rights. The requisite number of states ratified these amendments within two years of the adoption of the Constitution. A central obstacle to ratification of the Constitution was the absence of a bill of rights, a topic not discussed extensively at the Constitutional Convention in 1787[19] but one that subsequently became a major bone of contention when some Anti-Federalists sought either to convene a second convention or to ratify the Constitution conditionally. Seeking to head off these options, leading Federalists (especially James Madison)[20], agreed that if the Constitution were ratified, they would support the addition of a bill of rights.

The Bill of Rights undoubtedly grew out of distrust of the new government where the central government was to be much more powerful than that under the Articles of Confederation. In a sense, the most fascinating thing about the debate over the Bill of Rights was that both those who initially favored it and those who opposed it professed concern for protection of individual rights. Their central disagreement focused not on ends but on means.[21] Anti-Federalist proponents of the Bill of Rights thought that such guarantees as this bill embodied would be necessary to restrain the new central government.[22] Opponents argued that since the national government could only exercise powers which were granted to it, a bill of rights was simply superfluous.[23] Indeed, if the people came to regard such a bill of rights as an exhaustive listing, it could even become counterproductive in that people might assume that any rights not so listed were automatically forfeited.[24] This latter concern helps explain the adoption of the Ninth Amendment.[25] The Tenth Amendment served a similar purpose. While it is not altogether clear that Justice Stone's comment that the amendment "states but a truism that all is retained which has not been surrendered" would have been universally accepted among Federalists,[26] certainly many would have supported the idea that the amendment simply stated a relationship which already existed.

The guarantees in the Bill of Rights have had remarkable staying power.[27] As ratified, the Bill of Rights thus seems most clearly to fall on the right hand side of figure 2.1 as constituting a conservative or reactionary action. Those who initially favored the Bill of Rights saw these amendments as a way of either reversing or forestalling change. Those who initially opposed the amendments that became the Bill of Rights believed they simply preserved the status quo and were thus fairly harmless. If it were necessary to reassure the public by ratifying the Bill of Rights, Federalists were willing to do so.[28] As the authors of one book explain: "The first ten amendments confirmed, rather than revised, the conception of the American nation held by the American people between 1789 and 1791."[29]

THE ELEVENTH AND TWELFTH AMENDMENTS

Proponents of the Eleventh Amendment introduced it chiefly to reverse the Supreme Court's decision in *Chisholm v. Georgia* (1793) wherein the Court had declared that citizens from other states could sue state governments.[30] The Court's decision in *Chisholm* surprised many people because it contradicted specific assurances that some proponents of the Constitution had made in regard to states' sovereign immunity.[31] Given its relatively close proximity to the ratification of the Constitution, it therefore again is most logical to classify this amendment as a constitutional reversal or constitutional restoration. Undoubtedly, the Eleventh Amendment provided a change in the language of the Constitution, but proponents of this amendment instituted this change to return to a widespread understanding of what the Constitution originally meant rather than to institute a new understanding.[32] The wording of the amendment indicates that it was "intended to be read as a correction of a judicial misreading of an unaltered Constitution rather than a change of the Constitution to remove a disagreeable provision correctly interpreted by the Court."[33]

The Twelfth Amendment is more difficult to classify. On the surface, it ameliorated a defect in the original Constitution by seeking to prevent a tie in the electoral college (as had occurred in the presidential election of 1800) when candidates seeking the posts of president and vice president effectively ran on a party ticket. The Twelfth Amendment provided that electors would now separately cast votes for president and vice president.[34] The development of political parties had been unwelcome by most Founders and was probably unanticipated as well.[35] The Twelfth Amendment therefore appears to fall on the left side of figure 2.1, as an attempt either to sanction the development of the party system which had already occurred or to initiate a change to deal with an unanticipated development.

THE POST–CIVIL WAR AMENDMENTS

The nation adopted amendments Thirteen through Fifteen between 1865 and 1870. Each dealt in one way or another with the issues that had precipitated the Civil War. The Thirteenth Amendment abolished involuntary servitude, the Fourteenth Amendment extended citizenship to all natural-born Americans and attempted to guarantee certain fundamental rights to them, and the Fifteenth Amendment sought to prevent race from being used to deny the elective franchise.

Scholars generally regard the Civil War period and the amendments which followed as a time of profound change, what Bruce Ackerman identifies as a "constitutional moment."[36] Yet, particularly when set against the *Dred Scott* decision of 1857,[37] the Thirteenth and Fourteenth Amendments also represented a clear attempt to reverse an unpopular Supreme Court judgment.[38] In ruling that African-Americans could not be citizens, Chief Justice Taney had arguably given a more formal imprimatur to slavery than had the Constitution—which had always approached this issue with studied ambiguity. To the extent that citizenship and slavery are incompatible positions, the Thirteenth Amendment, like the Fourteenth, overturned the *Dred Scott* decision and thus belongs on the right side of figure 2.1. This is, however, clearly a case where the processes of reversing and initiating changes converge. To complicate matters still further, Lincoln had already issued his Emancipation Proclamation eliminating involuntary servitude, at least in Confederate territory. The effect of the Thirteenth Amendment was thus to extend, and undoubtedly to secure, actions which the executive branch had already initiated. In further putting nails in the coffin of the *Dred Scott* decision, the Fourteenth Amendment undoubtedly instituted, or sought to institute,[39] changes in the way that Americans treated a significant racial minority. The Fifteenth Amendment further attempted to guarantee the citizenship rights of black Americans by assuring their access to the polls. Significantly, the Fifteenth Amendment was the first of a number of attempts to guarantee voting rights (hitherto left to state discretion)[40] through federal constitutional amendment.

THE PROGRESSIVE ERA AMENDMENTS

The nation ratified four amendments between 1913 and 1920. The first, the Sixteenth, again shows how fine a line there is between reversing and initiating change, but it is probably best conceptualized as the former rather than the latter kind of alteration. During the Civil War, Congress had adopted and the Supreme Court had sanctioned a national income tax,[41] but, in the *Second Income Tax Case*, faced with allegations that the income tax was the first step down the road to socialism or communism,[42] the Court reversed its earlier course and declared that the income tax was the kind of "direct tax"[43] which could only be apportioned by population rather than by wealth or income.[44] By reversing this decision, the nation not only sanctioned a major source of revenue collection for the national government but also opened the way to use taxation as a way of redistributing wealth.

On their face, the Seventeenth through Nineteenth Amendments initiated major changes. The Seventeenth provided for direct election of Senators; the Eighteenth established national alcoholic prohibition; and the Nineteenth extended voting protection to American women.[45] While all three changes were indeed new to the federal Constitution, none was a completely new development, and there were states in which the amendments made absolutely no difference. Prior to the ratification of the Seventeenth Amendment, some state legislatures had already agreed to accept the people's choice as expressed in elections when selecting their Senators; to that extent, the amendment "codified in law a development—the democratization of the Senate—that already was settled fact."[46] Similarly, national alcoholic prohibition followed both upon national wartime alcoholic restrictions[47] and upon the adoption of numerous statewide prohibitions, especially in the South and the West.[48] The extension of voting rights to women also began at the state level in the West.[49] These facts do not detract from the achievements of any of these amendments, but they do indicate that changes may not always be quite as expansive as they appear to be on the surface.

AMENDMENTS TWENTY THROUGH TWENTY-SEVEN

It is not easy to group the amendments ratified since 1920 into clusters, and they are best evaluated individually. The Twentieth Amendment, which altered the inauguration date of the president and members of Congress, initiated a change designed, like a number of the Progressive Era amendments, to increase the accountability of office holders. The Twenty-First Amendment is *sui generis* in that it is the only amendment specifically designed to overturn another and thus to reverse a change previously initiated by amendment. A major impetus for this amendment was the widespread disobedience that faced the Eighteenth Amendment. In that respect, at least, the amendment did as much to sanction a change that had already occurred in public mores as it did to return to older conceptions of conduct and the appropriate limits of governmental regulation.

On the surface, the Twenty-Second Amendment which established a two-term or ten-year limit for presidents, clearly initiated a change in the formal Constitution. Indeed, this was a change that some had advocated almost from the beginning.[50] What probably took the wind out of the sails of those who favored this amendment, however, was the fact that from George Washington through Herbert Hoover, an informal understanding had developed that a president would step down at the end of his second term.[51] Franklin D. Roosevelt, of course, broke with this practice, and the Twenty-Second Amendment resurrected it. While thus inaugurating a change in the formal Constitution, the Twenty-Second Amendment actually reversed a change that had taken place in the informal constitution.

Amendments Twenty-Three through Twenty-Five all represent changes initiated by amendments. The Twenty-Third Amendment modified the electoral college and provided representation to residents of the District of Columbia. The Twenty-Fourth Amendment abolished the poll tax. While this amendment applied only to national elections, the Supreme Court subsequently outlawed poll taxes in state elections on the basis of the Equal Protection Clause of the Fourteenth Amendment.[52] This certainly suggests that the earlier change might also have been initiated short of amendment. Like the two prior amendments, the Twenty-Fifth altered the procedures both for declaring presidential disability and for filling vacancies in the vice presidency.

Like the Fifteenth and Nineteenth Amendments, the Twenty-Sixth Amendment extended national voting rights to a new class of citizens, namely, those from eighteen to twenty-one years old. Shortly before this amendment was proposed and ratified, the Supreme Court declared that a federal law designed to accomplish the same object could be applied only to national and not also to state elections.[53] In a sense, then, the Twenty-Sixth Amendment "reversed" a Supreme Court decision, but, given that there were no earlier conflicting interpretations (as there were in the case of the Eleventh, Fourteenth, and Sixteenth Amendments), the amendment did not so much represent the view that the Court's interpretation of the existing Constitution was wrong as it indicated that a majority of people preferred to have a Constitution which now provided differently.[54]

Of all the amendments ratified to date, the putative Twenty-Seventh Amendment has the most bizarre history. Originally, this amendment, which delays the implementation of any congressionally authorized pay raises for itself without an intervening election, was proposed as part of the bundle of amendments, ten of which became the Bill of Rights. The Twenty-Seventh amendment was not ratified, however, until 1992 after an aide to a Texas state legislator rediscovered it and served as a one-man crusader for its ratification.[55] Significantly, this amendment (like the other originally proposed as part of the Bill of Rights and still not ratified)[56] does not fit the model of the other provisions of the Bill of Rights in that rather than forestalling the national government from taking away civil liberties, it initiated a modification in the way that the government operated.

OTHER AMENDMENTS PROPOSED BY CONGRESS BUT UNRATIFIED

One problem with analyzing national constitutional amendments is that the number is small, only twenty-seven, with the first ten often cited as a single example. One way to remedy this problem is to look at some amendments which have been proposed but not ratified.

Altogether, Congress has proposed six amendments which were not ratified by the states. Like the amendment that in 1992 became the Twenty-Seventh to be ratified, one other was proposed along with the Bill of Rights. Like the Twenty-Seventh, it dealt not with the direct protection of individual civil liberties but rather with apportionment in Congress, guaranteeing at least one representative for every 30,000 people (the Constitution had specified that "the Number of Representatives shall not exceed one for every thirty Thousand")[57] until it had at least 100 members and at least one for each 40,000 persons up to 200 members.[58] This amendment would have clearly instituted a change in the Constitution.

In 1810, Congress proposed another still unratified amendment whose history and motivation are still fairly obscure.[59] This amendment would have made it illegal for any U.S. citizen, and not just for those who hold office,[60] to accept titles of nobility from abroad, and it would further have stripped citizenship from any individuals who accepted such titles. Although this changed the text of the Constitution, support for this amendment may have reflected some of the concerns initially expressed by Anti-Federalists that the new Constitution was establishing an aristocracy.

The period just before the U.S. Civil War spawned numerous plans to head off the crisis. The Corwin Amendment was one such plan.[61] In effect, this proposal sought to prohibit any future amendment which would interfere with the institution of slavery within any individual state. Had it been adopted, the Corwin Amendment would have preserved the status quo by attempting to forestall changes in the Constitution that might have threatened the South's "peculiar institution."

In 1924, Congress proposed an amendment "to limit, regulate, and prohibit the labor of persons under 18 years of age."[62] Previously, Congress had passed legislation under its authority to govern commerce among the states and under its taxing power, but the Supreme Court had struck down both efforts.[63] Advocates of the child labor amendment thus attempted to initiate a change through constitutional alteration that the Court declared they could not enact through legislation. Reported without a ratification deadline, the Supreme Court subsequently decided that it was the responsibility of Congress to decide on the timeliness of ratification of this amendment.[64] Although the necessary number of states never ratified this amendment, the Supreme Court ultimately reversed its earlier precedents and upheld national child labor legislation by approving the Fair Labor Standards Act of 1938.[65]

Necessary majorities of both houses of Congress proposed amendments in the 1970s, but both fell short of state ratification. One was the Equal Rights Amendment (ERA) designed to prevent a denial of "equality of rights under the law . . . on account of sex."[66] The arguments about this amendment were so diverse and strident that it is even today difficult to sort out the substantive aspects of the argument from the symbolic ones. Some argued that the amendment was basically meaningless because it would simply confirm expansive interpretations of gender rights already put in effect by the courts. Some argued, however, that such liberal decisions would be on surer footing if they were in the Constitution,[67] while others argued that there were some desirable changes which could not as effectively or as expansively be initiated without an amendment. Proponents of the former view saw the ERA as a way of sanctioning change, whereas advocates of the latter view emphasized the need to initiate still further change. Those who opposed the amendment generally associated it with changes that they did not desire. Ironically, congressional proposal of the amendment may have influenced judicial decision making in a pro-ERA direction even though the amendment itself was never ratified.[68]

In 1978, Congress proposed an amendment to treat the District of Columbia as a state for purposes of representation. This amendment is more clearly an attempt to initiate a change in the Constitution, albeit one necessitated by the unanticipated population growth in the area. The amendment failed largely because it promised greater advantage to one political party than to the other.[69]

ANALYSIS

Having now examined amendments which have been proposed by Congress by the necessary majorities, it is time to return to the five categories established previously to see what function most amendments have fulfilled. When so categorized, it is clear that most amendments serve more than one function. Thus the original line chart proves inadequate; a Venn diagram better captures this phenomenon. This is reproduced in Figure 2.2 with amendments categorized within the appropriate circles, and most, performing multiple functions, fall within the overlap of adjacent circles.

If Figure 2.2 is correct or largely so, a number of features seem especially important. In the first place, most amendments are indeed proposed by Congress in order to initiate change; they are found in circle D. Such amendments were ratified as early as 1795 and as recently as 1992, and they span most of America's constitutional history. For some amendments, initiating change seems to be their central focus. These would include the Twentieth Amendment, the Twenty-Third, the Twenty-Fourth, the Twenty-Fifth, the Twenty-Seventh, and the proposed amendment to provide congressional representation for the District of Columbia. All such amendments fall within the last six decades, suggesting, but surely not proving, that as a Constitution gets older, more amendments might be seen as desirable.

Some of these legal changes which the amending process has initiated can be interpreted to sanction changes which have already taken place and therefore fall in the overlap between circles D and E. Thus, while changing the language of the Constitution, the Twelfth Amendment gave some sanction to the developing party system. In permanently abolishing slavery, the Thirteenth Amendment extended the earlier Emancipation Proclamation. The Seventeenth, Nineteenth, and Twenty-Sixth Amendments followed earlier precedents in some of the states by extending the elective franchise. Proponents of the Equal Rights Amendment viewed it in part as a way of permanently securing legal rights recently won in the courts.

Another subset of amendments designed to initiate change did so by reversing changes, thus falling within the overlap of circles C and D. These include the Eleventh, the Fourteenth, the Sixteenth, and the Twenty-Second, the first three reversing Supreme Court decisions and the last reversing a change which had occurred in the nation's customs and usages. The Twenty-Sixth Amendment may be grouped with the Eleventh, Fourteenth, and Sixteenth Amendments to the extent that it

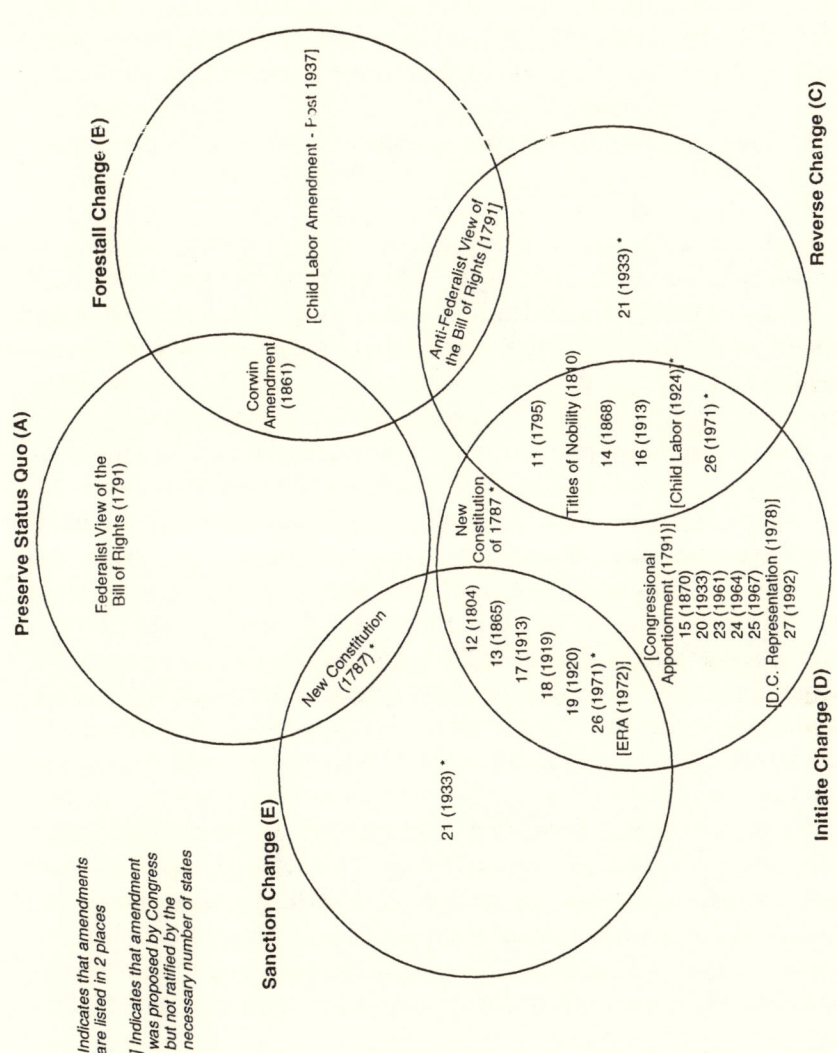

Figure 2.2
Constitutional Amendments

sought to reverse a Supreme Court decision, albeit one that did not come as the same legal surprise that the others had.

The only amendment which has been specifically ratified in order to reverse another was the Twenty-First Amendment repealing prohibition in 1933. When understood as simply recognizing an alteration in mores which had already taken place (or as recognizing that some mores were beyond the scope of legal coercion), however, this amendment also sanctioned a change already in progress.

It is difficult to find an amendment designed simply to forestall change, although, to turn to a not altogether hypothetical example, it is certainly not inconceivable that some individuals would have continued to push for a child-labor amendment even after the Court had given child labor legislation sanction, for fear that such a decision was not permanent. There are, however, amendments which clearly sought to forestall change while thus reversing change or preserving the status quo. In the first category, symbolized in figure 2.2 by the intersection of circles B and C, are the first eight amendments, at least as these amendments were understood by their original Anti-Federalist proponents. The proposed Corwin Amendment seems to fit more clearly in the second category, the overlap of circles A and B, attempting to preserve the Union (then the status quo) by preventing northern states from interfering with the institution of slavery. Since neither the Corwin Amendment nor the Child Labor Amendment was adopted, the only use of the amending process to forestall change thus remains the Bill of Rights, now over 200 years old.

As indicated at the beginning of this chapter, the people are unlikely to wield the heavy amending mechanisms simply to preserve the status quo, but certainly some groups of individuals may choose not to oppose an amendment desired by others simply because they do not believe that the amendments will make a significant difference one way or another. Such, this author suggests, was the eventual Federalist attitude toward the Bill of Rights. The Ninth and Tenth Amendments, in particular, seem simply to restate the Federalist views of state and individual rights without thereby attempting to change them. While it is not so classified on the chart, some people may have taken a similar attitude toward the proposed Equal Rights Amendment.

Of the amendments proposed by Congress, none appear to fit the overlap between circles A and E. There is an element of contradiction between sanctioning change and preserving the status quo, but it is certainly possible to imagine a situation where an amendment is ratified with the purpose of giving formal sanction to a change which has already been initiated by another branch of government. Thus, an amendment providing national protection to the right to choose an abortion would essentially preserve the status quo as it has been established by *Roe v. Wade* and its progeny.

Not surprisingly, however, the central historical function of amendments has been to initiate change. Amendments have played particularly important roles in extending voting and other civil rights, in making minor alterations in governmental structures and mechanisms,[70] and in reversing, or attempting to reverse, unpopular Supreme Court decisions. Not since the Bill of Rights has the nation ratified an amendment or set of amendments simply to preserve the status quo or forestall change. While the amending process is thus chiefly an agent of change, the people may just as easily use it to return the nation to a past practice or to sanction or extend a change that has already begun within the states or elsewhere in the political system as to inaugurate something new under the sun.

NOTES

1. Robert Nisbet, *History of the Idea of Progress* (New York: Basic Books, 1980). For reflections on the influence of this idea on the Warren Court, see Alexander M. Bickel, *The Supreme Court and the Idea of Progress* (New Haven, CT: Yale University Press, 1978).

2. See Woodrow Wilson's contrast between the Newtonian and Darwinian models of a Constitution in *Constitutional Government in the United States* (New York: Columbia University Press, 1961; reprint of 1908 edition), pp. 25–45. This link to Darwinism is discussed in Thomas H. Peebles, "A Call to High Debate: The Organic Constitution in Its Formative Era, 1890–1920," *University of Colorado Law Review* 52 (Fall 1980), pp. 49–104.

3. Thus, Alan P. Grimes links the amending process to the expansion of American democracy. See his *Democracy and the Amendments to the Constitution* (Lexington, MA: Lexington Books, 1978).

4. D. O. McGovney, "Is the Eighteenth Amendment Void Because of Its Contents?" *Columbia Law Review* 20 (May 1920), p. 514.

5. One could, of course, attempt further to "entrench" a constitutional provision by making it more difficult to change. Currently, the only applicable entrenchment provision of the U.S. Constitution prohibits a state from being deprived of its suffrage in the U.S. Senate without its consent. Just before the U.S. Civil War, there were attempts to entrench the institution of slavery through the so-called Corwin Amendment which was proposed as part of the Crittenden Compromise. See Stephen Keogh, "Formal and Informal Constitutional Lawmaking in the United States in the Winter of 1860–1861," *Journal of Legal History* 8 (December 1987), pp. 275–99 and R. Alton Lee, "The Corwin Amendment in the Secession Crisis," *Ohio Historical Quarterly* 70 (January 1961), pp. 1–26.

6. Existing jurisprudence in this area was, of course, initiated by the decision in *Roe v. Wade*, 410 U.S. 113 (1973).

7. See Jer. 7:3, 5; Jer. 26:13 (AV). In the King James version, in John 4:52, the word *amend* is used to describe a person getting well, as in the contemporary phrase indicating that someone is "on the mend."

8. This was, of course, the Twenty-First Amendment which abolished national alcoholic prohibition as established in the Eighteenth Amendment.

9. Thus, one modern critic of judicial activism has argued that one result of such activism has been that most modern amending proposals have been designed not "to *reform* the Constitution" but rather "to *restore* a Constitution modified by means other than Article V." See Stephen J. Markman, "The Jurisprudence of Constitutional Amendments," in *Still the Law of the Land?*, ed. Joseph S. McNamara and Lissa Roche (Hillsdale, MI: Hillsdale College Press, 1987), p. 90.

10. 410 U.S. 113 (1973).

11. This writer has dealt with the subject in *A Companion to the United States Constitution and Its Amendments* (Westport, CT: Praeger, 1993), pp. 1–21.

12. Words taken from the congressional resolution of February 21, 1787 as found in *The Federal Convention and the Formation of the Union of the American States*, ed. Winton U. Solberg (New York: Liberal Arts Press, 1958), p. 64.

13. Vile, *A Companion to the U.S. Constitution*, pp. 91–92.

14. Ibid., p. 51. Constitution of the Articles of Confederation.

15. This author therefore agrees with Richard S. Kay's argument that the new Constitution was illegal (albeit no less legitimate on that account). See Kay's article, "The Illegality of the Constitution," *Constitutional Commentary* 4 (Winter 1987), pp. 57–80.

16. *The Federalist Papers*, ed. Clinton Rossiter (New York: New American Library, 1961), p. 248.

17. Ibid., p. 251.

18. Ibid., p. 254.

19. Ralph Ketcham, *Framed for Posterity: The Enduring Philosophy of the Constitution* (Lawrence: University Press of Kansas, 1993), p. 87.

20. For Madison's role, see William L. Miller, *The Business of May Next: James Madison and the Founding* (Charlottesville: University Press of Virginia, 1992), pp. 235–59.

21. Ketcham, *Framed for Posterity*, p. 88.

22. Ibid., p. 93.

23. Ibid., p. 92.

24. Vile, *A Companion to the United States Constitution*, p. 151.

25. For a more complete analysis of this amendment, see *The Rights Retained by the People: The History and Meaning of the Ninth Amendment*, ed. Randy E. Barnette (Fairfax, VA: George Mason University Press, 1989).

26. *United States v. Darby Lumber Company*, 312 U.S. 100 (1941), p. 124.

27. John R. Vile, "Proposals to Amend the Bill of Rights: Are Fundamental Rights in Jeopardy?" *Judicature* 75 (August–September 1991), pp. 62–67.

28. Ketcham, *Framed for Posterity*, p. 99, thus notes that "Madison's support for a bill of rights, though entirely sincere in substance, continued to be phrased in tactical terms."

29. Richard B. Bernstein with Jerome Agel, *Amending America: If We Love the Constitution So Much, Why Do We Keep Trying to Change It?* (New York: Random House, 1993), p. 47.

30. 2 Dallas 419 (1793).

31. Alpheus T. Mason and Donald G. Stephenson, Jr., *American Constitutional Law*, 10th ed. (Englewood Cliffs, NJ: Prentice-Hall, 1993), p. 157.

32. H. Jefferson Powell thus notes that in the early years of the republic, "For Congress, at least, the legislative role in proposing constitutional amendments often was seen as a special subset of the general legislative duty to interpret the Constitution." Powell notes that Madison regarded the Bill of Rights as "explanatory amendments" and that Thomas M'Kean viewed the Eleventh Amendment as a "legislative declaration of the meaning of the constitution." See Powell's, "The Political Grammar of Early Constitutional Law," *North Carolina Law Review* 71 (April 1993), p. 976.

33. Bernstein with Agel, *Amending America*, p. 56.

34. See John J. Turner, Jr., "The Twelfth Amendment and the First American Party System," *The Historian* 35 (1973), pp. 221–37 and Richard B. Bernstein, "Fixing the Electoral College," *Constitution* 5 (Winter 1993), pp. 42–48.

35. Richard Hofstader, *The Idea of a Party System: The Rise of Legitimate Opposition in the United States, 1780–1840* (Berkeley: University of California Press, 1972).

36. Ackerman also refers to such times as periods of "higher lawmaking." See *We the People: Foundations* (Cambridge, MA: Harvard University Press, Belknap Press, 1991), pp. 266–94.

37. *Dred Scott v. Sandford*, 19 Howard (60 U.S.) 393 (1857).

38. There is, of course, continuing dispute as to whether the privileges and immunities or the due process clause of the Fourteenth Amendment was specifically formulated to reverse the Supreme Court's decision in *Barron v. Baltimore*, 32 U.S. 243 (1833) and apply the provisions of the Bill of Rights to the states. For one of the best-known discussions on the Supreme Court of this issue, see the exchange between Justices Felix Frankfurter and Hugo Black in *Adamson v. California*, 332 U.S. 46 (1947). For a recent piece which gives credence to the view that key supporters of the Fourteenth Amendment, especially Representative John Bingham, had his purpose in mind, see Richard L. Aynes, "On Misreading John Bingham and the Fourteenth Amendment," *The Yale Law Journal* 103 (October 1993), pp. 57–104.

39. The early promise of the post–Civil War Amendments was to a large extent eviscerated by discriminatory state actions and by subsequent Court decisions, most notably in *The Slaughterhouse Cases*, 83 U.S. 36 (1873), *The Civil Rights Cases of 1883*, 109 U.S. 3 (1883), and in *Plessy v. Ferguson*, 163 U.S. 537 (1896). Such interpretations are discussed in Howard Jay Graham's, *Everyman's Constitution: Historical Essays on the Fourteenth Amendment, the "Conspiracy The-*

ory," and American Constitutionalism (Madison: State Historical Society of Wisconsin, 1968). For a recent study detailing how the idea of substantive due process was read into the Fourteenth Amendment, see Richard C. Cortner, *The Iron Horse and the Constitution: The Railroads and the Transformation of the Fourteenth Amendment* (Westport, CT: Greenwood Press, 1993).

40. Note, however, the never enforced punitive provisions of Section 2 of the Fourteenth Amendment for states who denied the vote on the basis of race.

41. *Springer v. United States,* 102 U.S. 586 (1881).

42. Joseph Choate thus argued before the Court that the tax was "communistic in its purposes and tendencies, and is defended here upon principles as communistic, socialistic—what shall I call them—populistic as ever have been addressed to any political assembly in the world." See Melvin I. Urofsky, *A March of Liberty: A Constitutional History of the United States* (New York: Alfred A. Knopf, 1988), p. 537.

43. The language is from Article I, Section 9 of the U.S. Constitution.

44. *Pollock v. Farmers' Loan & Trust Co.,* 158 U.S. 601 (1895).

45. The Supreme Court had ruled in *Minor v. Happersett,* 21 Wall. (88 U.S.) 162 (1875), that such voting rights had not been extended by the Fourteenth Amendment.

46. Bernstein with Agel, *Amending America,* p. 126.

47. See Christopher N. May, *In the Name of War* (Cambridge, MA: Harvard University Press, 1989).

48. Alan P. Grimes, *Democracy and the Amendments to the Constitution* (Lexington, MA: Lexington Books, 1978), pp. 84–85.

49. Bernstein with Agel, *Amending America,* p. 132.

50. Thomas Jefferson was among those who had favored rotation in the presidential office. See Dumas Malone, *Jefferson and the Rights of Man* (Boston: Little, Brown and Company, 1951), p. 168.

51. Christopher G. Tiedeman, *The Unwritten Constitution of the United States* (New York: G. P. Putnam's Sons, 1890), pp. 51–54, cited this custom as part of America's unwritten Constitution. Herbert W. Horwill, *The Usages of the American Constitution* (Port Washington, NY: Kennikat Press, 1969 reissue of 1925), pp. 88–100, discusses the two-term limit but is less certain how strong the custom was likely to continue to be.

52. *Harper v. Virginia State Board of Elections,* 383 U.S. 663 (1966).

53. *Oregon v. Mitchell,* 400 U.S. 112 (1970).

54. Ruth Bader Ginsberg, "On Amending the Constitution: A Plea for Patience," *University of Arkansas at Little Rock Law Journal* 12 (1989–90), p. 688.

55. For a more complete accounting of this amendment, see Richard B. Bernstein, "The Sleeper Wakes: The History and Legacy of the Twenty-Seventh Amendment," *Fordham Law Review* 61 (December 1992), pp. 497–557. The process by which this amendment was putatively ratified some 200 years after being proposed has been subject to a devastating critique by William Van Alstyne in "What Do You Think About the Twenty-Seventh Amendment?" *Constitu-*

tional Commentary 10 (Winter 1993, pp. 9–18. Also see Sanford Levinson, "On the Constitution's Text: The Problem of the (So-Called) Twenty-Seventh Amendment," scheduled for tenth anniversary issue of *Constitutional Commentary*; Ruth Ann Strickland, "The Twenty-Seventh Amendment and Constitutional Change by Stealth," *PS: Political Science & Politics* 26 (December 1993), pp. 716–22; Christopher M. Kennedy, "Is There a Twenty-Seventh Amendment? The Unconstitutionality of a 'New' 203-Year-Old Amendment," *The John Marshall Law Review* 26 (September 1993), pp. 977–1019; and Michael S. Paulsen, "A General Theory of Article V: The Constitutional Lessons of the Twenty-Seventh Amendment," *The Yale Law Journal* 103 (December 1993), pp. 677–789.

56. This amendment dealt with representation in Congress. For analysis, see Akil R. Amar, "The Bill of Rights as a Constitution," *Yale Law Journal* 100 (Winter 1992), pp. 1137–146.

57. Article I, Section 2 [3].

58. For text of amendment, see Appendix L, George Anastaplo, *The Constitution of 1787: A Commentary* (Baltimore, MD: Johns Hopkins University Press, 1989), pp. 198–99.

59. Bernstein with Agel, *Amending America*, pp. 177–78.

60. See Article I, Section 9 [8].

61. See R. Alton Lee, "The Corwin Amendment in the Secession Crisis," *Ohio Historical Quarterly* 70 (January 1961), pp. 1–26 and Stephen Keogh, "Formal and Informal Constitutional Lawmaking in the United States in the Winter of 1860–1861," *Journal of Legal History* 8 (1987), pp. 275–99.

62. For an expanded history of this controversy, see Stephen B. Wood, *Constitutional Politics in the Progressive Era: Child Labor and the Law* (Chicago: University of Chicago Press, 1968).

63. *Hammer v. Dagenhart*, 247 U.S. 251 (1918) and *Bailey v. Drexel Furniture Company*, 259 U.S. 20 (1922).

64. *Coleman v. Miller*, 307 U.S. 433 (1939). Also see *Chandler v. Wise*, 307 U.S. 474 (1939).

65. *United States v. Darby Lumber Company*, 312 U.S. 100 (1941).

66. Among the best discussions of this failed proposal are Jane J. Mansbridge, *Why We Lost the ERA* (Chicago: University of Chicago Press, 1986), and Mary F. Berry, *Why ERA Failed* (Bloomington: Indiana University Press, 1986).

67. Jennifer K. Brown has recently added an interesting twist to this argument by suggesting that rather than being interpreted strictly as dealing with women's suffrage, the Nineteenth Amendment "can and should be recognized as an affirmation of women's constitutional equality." See "The Nineteenth Amendment and Women's Equality," *The Yale Law Journal* 102 (June 1993), p. 2175.

68. Leslie F. Goldstein, "The ERA and the U.S. Supreme Court," *Research in Law and Policy Studies*, vol. 1, ed. Stuart S. Nagel (Greenwich, CT: JAI Press, 1987), pp. 145–61.

69. Clement Vose, "When District of Columbia Representation Collides with the Constitutional Amendment Institution," *Publius: The Journal of Federalism* 9

(Winter 1979), pp. 105–25. Also see Dottie Horn, "Another Star for the Stripes?" *Endeavors* 8 (Fall 1990), pp. 4–6.

70. This is consistent with the classification scheme used by Ruth A. Strickland, "Population Size, Diversity and the Proclivity of States to Oppose or Support the Ratification of Amendments to the U.S. Constitution," *Southeastern Political Review* 20 (Fall 1992), pp. 271–74.

Chapter 3

A Selective Look at
Supreme Court Decisions
and Their Impact on Change

While the difficulty of constitutional amendment has undoubtedly contributed to the stability of the written instrument, this difficulty has also created pressure to effect constitutional changes by other less onerous means consistent with the spirit, if not specified in the letter, of the Constitution.[1] Key among such means is the mechanism of judicial review. The beauty of judicial review is not simply that it can provide a means of giving authoritative interpretations of the Constitution but also that it can overcome the rigidity seemingly inherent in the unchanging words of the Constitutional text. If history be any guide on this matter, there is little that constitutional amendments can do that judicial review cannot do, if not better at least with the expenditure of less energy.

When compared to Figure 2.1, Figure 3.1 should suggest the parallels between judicial review and constitutional amendment:

Judicial Interpretations can:

Initiate Change	Sanction Change	Preserve Status Quo	Forestall Change	Reverse Change

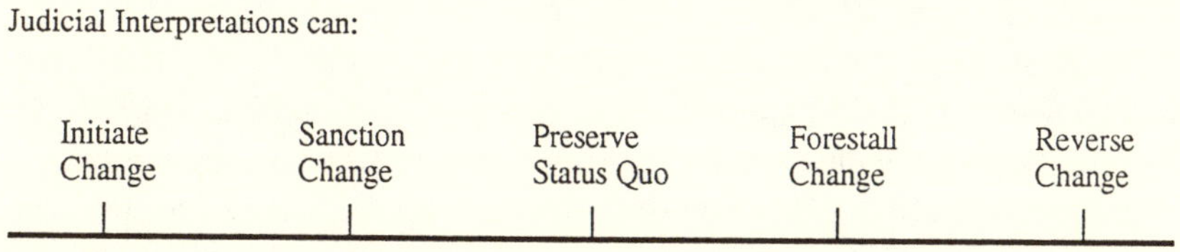

Figure 3.1
Judicial Interpretation and Change

Whereas a central problem in analyzing constitutional amendments is the paucity of amendments that have been proposed by the requisite majorities of Congress and ratified by the states, the problem in analyzing Supreme Court decisions is that there are so many of them, and they are spread over such a long time period that any manageable list is likely to be arbitrary. Accordingly, in the pages below, decisions are selected to illustrate occasions when the Supreme Court has performed each of the designated functions.[2]

COURT DECISIONS DESIGNED TO PRESERVE
THE STATUS QUO

Whereas it is fairly unusual to think of an amendment to the Constitution being ratified simply to preserve the status quo, this is probably the most common function of judicial review. Particularly in traditional legal theory, the function of the judge was to "declare" the law, not to "make" or initiate it.[3] About the most that this older view would concede was that in the absence of clear precedents the Court would sometimes have to "interpret" existing law.

Over the last two centuries, the Supreme Court has rendered tens of thousands of decisions. Yet during this time, it has reversed just over 140 federal laws in whole or in part and only 1,200 provisions in state laws and constitutions.[4] These figures suggest that in most cases where the Court confronts state or federal initiatives, it defers to the judgments of constitutionality that were made when such laws were adopted.

Similarly, the Court frequently utilizes the hoary doctrine of *stare decisis* and applies existing precedents. The strength, albeit not necessarily the wisdom, of this doctrine is perhaps most evident in those cases where the Court continues with an existing precedent which is in tension with others. In *Flood v. Kuhn* (1972), for example, in the face of congressional inaction in the aftermath of earlier decisions, Justice Blackmun wrote a decision for the Court ruling that—unlike boxing, football, and basketball—baseball would not be considered as being in interstate commerce and subject to the provisions of the Sherman Antitrust Act.[5] Similarly, while striking down a sexually discriminatory law in *Frontiero v. Richardson* (1973), the four justices who wanted to have gender declared a suspect category ran into Justice Powell's objection (expressed in a concurring opinion) that since the Equal Rights Amendment was then pending and might substantially accomplish the same object, the better course of action would be for the Court to wait:

The Equal Rights Amendment, which if adopted will resolve the substance of this precise question, has been approved by the Congress and submitted for ratification by the States. If this Amendment is duly adopted, it will represent the will of the people accomplished in the manner prescribed by the Constitution. By acting prematurely and unnecessarily, as I view it, the Court has assumed a decisional responsibility at the very time when state legislatures, functioning within the traditional democratic process, are debating the proposed amendment. It seems to me that this reaching out to pre-empt by judicial action a major political decision which is currently in process of resolution does not reflect appropriate respect for duly prescribed legislative processes.[6]

One of the Court's most fascinating recent discussions of the doctrine of *stare decisis* is found in *Planned Parenthood v. Casey* (1992),[7] when it decided to accept certain restrictions on abortion without thereby overturning the central holding in *Roe v. Wade*[8] that a woman had a constitutional right to procure an abortion.[9] In an opinion Justices O'Connor, Kennedy, and Souter devoted a full seven to eight pages to the value, albeit a value that could sometimes be outweighed, of adhering to existing precedents.[10]

The three justices argued that in deciding to reverse earlier opinions the Court must weigh the need for "continuity over time" against the possibility that an earlier precedent was "so clearly [viewed] as error that its enforcement was for that very reason doomed."[11] In examining the Court's bellwether abortion decision in *Roe v. Wade*, the justices argued that four considerations were prominent:

whether *Roe's* central rule has been found unworkable; whether the rule's limitation on state power could be removed without serious inequity to those who have relied upon it or significant damage to the stability of the society governed by the rule in question; whether the law's growth in the intervening years has left *Roe's* central rule a doctrinal anachronism discounted by society; and whether *Roe's* premises of fact have so far changed in the ensuing two decades as to render its central holding somehow irrelevant or unjustifiable in dealing with the issue it addressed.[12]

Finding the answer to each of these questions to be negative, the three justices attempted to distinguish their decision not to overturn *Roe v. Wade* from two prominent other decisions, represented by *West Coast Hotel v. Parrish* (1937)[13] and *Brown v. Board of Education* (1954).[14] In the case at hand, the justices argued, a reversal would exact a "terrible price"[15] since, absent changes in circumstances, the Court would have difficulty persuading the public that its reversal was "grounded truly in principle" rather than "as compromises with social and political pressures having, as such, no bearing on the principled choices that the Court is obliged to make."[16] The justices further argued that the original decision in *Roe*, like only one other in their lifetime (that being *Brown v. Board*), had specifically attempted to "resolve the sort of intensely divisive controversy" which required that "its decision has a dimension that the resolution of the normal case does not carry."[17] They concluded that *stare decisis* was important, albeit not sacrosanct: "The promise of constancy, once given, binds its maker for as long as the power to stand by the decision survives and the understanding of the issue has not changed so fundamentally as to render the commitment obsolete."[18]

COURT DECISIONS FORESTALLING CHANGE

As was the case in the discussion of constitutional amendments, there is a fine line between decisions intended to preserve the status quo and those intended to forestall or prevent change, but some decisions do appear to fall more clearly in the latter category than in the former. In describing such cases, it is useful to distinguish those decisions designed to forestall changes in the power and/or composition of the Court from those which are designed to forestall, or have the effect of forestalling, changes in the Constitution.

Decisions Forestalling Changes That Would Weaken the Court

If it is not altogether true that Supreme Court decisions follow the election returns, it is certainly evident that the Supreme Court is a highly political institution whose members are appointed by the president and confirmed by the Senate and who are likely to place a fairly high premium on institutional survival. While it would undoubtedly be difficult or impossible to establish a direct causation, there are certainly examples where judicial flexibility has contributed to the Court's survival. Thus, while Chief Justice John Marshall asserted a strong right of judicial review of national legislation in *Marbury v. Madison* (1803), he also avoided a direct confrontation with Jefferson (who had vigorously criticized the Court and pushed for the impeachment of Justice Chase)[19] and thus sidestepped further efforts at judicial restrictions by declaring that the Court did not have authority in this case to issue a writ of mandamus compelling delivery of Marbury's commission.[20] Similarly, in reversing course in 1937 with *National Labor Relations Board v. Jones & Laughlin Steel Corp.* (1937),[21] the Supreme Court undeniably took away the primary impetus for passage of Franklin Roosevelt's "court-packing plan."[22]

Because the members of the Court are political appointees, new members often—though not inevitably—reflect the ideological predispositions of those who appoint and confirm them.[23] Ironically, then, by adapting to popular concerns about the direction of the Court, new justices make other forms of political retaliation less likely. President Nixon's promise to appoint "strict constructionists" to the Court who would "strengthen the peace forces as against the criminal forces of the land"[24] undoubtedly relieved pressure on the Court that had been building with the unsuccessful movement to impeach Chief Justice Earl Warren. Appointments by Reagan and Bush probably had a similar impact on attempts to limit judicial jurisdiction over such areas as abortion or civil rights.

Decisions Forestalling Changes in the Constitution

Just as judicial decisions may forestall the progress of attacks on the Court as an institution, so too decisions might stymie efforts at formal constitutional amendment. Although this seems more clearly an unintended effect than a clear intention, when in 1941 the Supreme Court invalidated earlier precedents and upheld a child labor law, it therefore largely undercut any sentiment that remained for adoption of a child labor amendment.[25] The Supreme Court's decision in *Reid v. Covert* (1957)[26] which invalidated an executive agreement providing for military trials of civilian defendants of those in the U.S. military may also have placated some of the fears reflected in the failed Bricker Amendment.[27] Similarly, some observers believe that the Court's increasingly liberal view of women's rights under the Equal Protection Clause did more to hinder the Equal Rights Amendment than to aid in its ratification. At one and the same time, liberal decisions allowed some to argue that the amendment was no longer needed and would make no real difference just as others could hint darkly of what the Court might do with yet another broad phrase in their constitutional arsenal. Supreme Court decisions which limited the scope of school busing,[28] sanctioned extracurricular religious activities in public schools,[29] and allowed for greater state restrictions on the right to abortion[30] might similarly have undermined support for amendments designed to address each of these areas.

COURT DECISIONS REVERSING CHANGE

In looking at judicial decisions which have reversed changes, it is wise to distinguish at the outset among a number of possibilities. At least four seem to stand out. A Court decision can reverse a decision it has rendered itself; it can reverse or modify a change previously effected by constitutional amendment; it can reverse a change that has been enacted by law or executive order; or it can reverse a change that has come about by customs and usages.

Reversing Decisions by the Court

Despite occasional paeans to the doctrine of *stare decisis,* many Court decisions have overturned previous rulings,[31] and there is a sense in which every dissenting opinion is an appeal for such reversals.[32] While acknowledging the difficulty of making a precise count, one writer says there were more than 100 such decisions from 1810 to 1973;[33] another writer notes 106 cases involving constitutional interpretation where "the Supreme Court made unmistakably clear its intent to overrule some prior decision(s)."[34]

Moreover, such decisions are often major ones which receive considerable attention.[35] Certainly, the Court's decision in *Brown v. Board of Education* (1954),[36] overturning the doctrine of "separate but equal" which had been established in *Plessy v. Ferguson* (1896),[37] is one of the most important decisions of this century.[38] Similarly, in *Baker v. Carr* (1962),[39] the Supreme Court reversed its earlier stance in *Colegrove v. Green* (1946)[40] and decided that issues involving state legislative apportionment would now be justiciable. A much quicker reversal occurred in *West Virginia State Board of Education v. Barnette* (1943)[41] where the Supreme Court overturned a decision rendered just three years earlier in *Minersville School District v. Gobitis* (1940).[42] In *Katz v. United States* (1967),[43] the Court overturned its decision in *Olmstead v. United States* (1928)[44] and declared that warrantless wiretaps were unconstitutional. In *Gideon v. Wainwright* (1963),[45] the Supreme Court reversed its decision in *Betts v. Brady* (1942)[46] and ruled that indigent defendants were entitled to court-appointed attorneys even in non-capital cases where there were no extraordinary circumstances present. Similarly, in *Payne v. Tennessee* (1991),[47] the Supreme Court reversed earlier rulings in *Booth v. Maryland* (1987)[48] and *South Carolina v. Gathers* (1989)[49] and declared that victim impact statements could now be used in the sentencing phase of a criminal trial. With such examples in mind, on May 31, 1984 a group called Americans United for Life sponsored a conference entitled "Reversing *Roe v. Wade* Through the Courts," which they subsequently embodied in a book.[50]

Reversing Constitutional Amendments

While it is common to think of amendments being proposed to reverse Supreme Court decisions, at least at the national level, it is perhaps less common to think of Court decisions which reverse amendments. In recent years, however, there has been considerable writing by those, generally of a "liberal" political persuasion, who argue that it is possible to imagine an "unconstitutional" amendment and that, in such circumstances, it would be the duty of the Court to void such an alteration.[51] The fact that these arguments are not merely theoretical is established by the fact that the Court was asked by leading conservatives much earlier in this century to invalidate a number of amendments on precisely these grounds.[52] While the Supreme Court of the United States has never accepted such an invitation to activism,[53] and, in this author's opinion, should never do so, this is at least a theoretical possibility.

If the Supreme Court has never declared an amendment unconstitutional, however, it surely has interpreted some amendments in a restrictive fashion which suggests a negative animus toward their broad purposes. The premier example is most surely the Fourteenth Amendment, although it is difficult to be overly dogmatic about the effect of Court decisions given the decided ambiguity that appears to have motivated those who proposed and ratified this amendment.[54] To the extent the Supreme Court erred in interpreting this amendment, it certainly erred, however, in giving it too conservative a reading. In its earliest decision on the Fourteenth Amendment, the so-called *Slaughterhouse Cases* (1873), the Supreme Court was particularly candid in expressing its own reluctance to interpret the amendment in an expansive fashion. Justice Miller thus stated:

> The argument we admit is not always the most conclusive which is drawn from the consequences urged against the adoption of a particular construction of an instrument. But when, as in the case before us, these consequences are so serious, so far reaching and pervading, so great a departure from the structure and spirit of our institution . . . the argument has a force that is irresistible, in the absence of language which expresses such a purpose too clearly to admit of doubt.[55]

Taking such a conservative approach to judicial interpretation, the Court effectively eviscerated the privileges and immunities clause so as to apply only to a small number of rights identified as national in scope.

The *Civil Rights Cases* (1883)[56] and *Plessy v. Ferguson* (1896)[57] had similar impacts. In the first case, the Court narrowed the scope of the Fourteenth Amendment by focusing on the "state action" requirement. In the second, it lessened the potential impact of the equal protection clause by permitting segregation in cases where separate facilities were equal.[58] Much later, of course, the Court reversed direction in *Brown v. Board of Education*.

Reversing Laws or Executive Orders

Certainly, the most awesome function that U.S. courts perform is the exercise of judicial review wherein they declare that state or federal laws or executive orders are void because they are contrary to the Constitution. Typically, one would expect that the Court might show deference here to the decisions of the politically elected branches as it professed to do when in *Rostker v. Goldberg* (1981) it refused to overrule the congressional judgment that registration for selective service should apply to males but not to females. In that case, the Court noted that "the customary deference accorded the judgments of Congress is certainly appropriate when, as here, Congress specifically considered the question of the act's constitutionality."[59] Throughout American history, the U.S. Supreme Court has declared just over 140 laws or parts of laws unconstitutional, with 69 of these decisions occurring since 1937.[60] At the state level it has voided approximately 1,200 laws or state constitutional provisions, with approximately 850 of these decisions occurring since 1870.[61] Since most laws or executive orders are enacted in order to effect change or to validate existing customs, Court decisions voiding laws have the effect of reversing such changes.

Thus, in *Hammer v. Dagenhart* (1918), the Supreme Court voided the Keating-Owen Child Labor Law of 1916, ruling that Congress could not impose national child-labor legislation on the basis of the interstate commerce clause,[62] a decision widened in *Bailey v. Drexel Furniture Company* (1922)[63] when the Court subsequently decided that Congress could not accomplish the same objective through the taxing power.[64] Likewise, in the *Steel Seizure Case*, the Supreme Court ruled that President Truman's actions in seizing the steel mills in order to avert a threatened strike were unconstitutional.[65] Similarly, in *Griswold v. Connecticut* (1965), the Supreme Court overturned a Connecticut law which prohibited the use or distribution of birth control devices,[66] and, in *Roe v. Wade*, it declared Texas's antiabortion laws to be unconstitutional.[67] In *Texas v. Johnson* (1989), the Supreme Court struck down a Texas law making it illegal to burn an American flag,[68] and, in *United States v. Eichman* (1990), the Supreme Court struck down a federal law designed for a similar purpose.[69] Given the nature of the American constitutional system, each time the courts strike down a law on constitutional grounds, it is indicating that the change cannot be accomplished, short of constitutional amendment or a reversal or modification in the Court's own stance.

Reversing Customs and Usages

Customs and usages which grow up outside of the constitutional text may or may not be embodied into law. On many, if not most, occasions that the courts review such customs, they probably end up validating them.[70] Certainly, one such custom which was not so validated was the so-called legislative veto whereby the president—often under protest—received authority over a given area of law subject to veto by the vote of one or both houses of Congress. Even though this practice had been in use for several decades, the Supreme Court finally declared the procedure illegal in the *Chadha Case*,[71] thus practically forcing the legislative and executive branches to seek accommodations in other ways.

The Supreme Court arguably struck at another developing custom and usage in *United States v. Nixon* (1974) when, while not voiding the idea of executive privilege outright, it indicated that the privilege was considerably less extensive than the use President Nixon desired to make of it.[72] Similarly, while many assumed that the custom of unanimous verdicts and of twelve-member juries were implicit in the Bill of Rights, the Supreme Court ruled that these widespread practices, while certainly permitted, were not mandated by the constitutional text.[73] Likewise, in *Rutan v. Republican Party of Illinois* (1990), the Supreme Court significantly curtailed the long-standing use of party patronage in hiring, promotions, and transfers.[74]

COURT DECISIONS SANCTIONING CHANGE

While judicial power tends to be defined in terms of judicial review and thus in terms of the laws it overturns, judicial power may be far more important in sanctioning and legitimizing laws than in overturning them.[75] Since there are literally thousands of examples of such decisions, it is, again, fairly difficult to know which to choose for discussion.

Certainly, one case that belongs in almost every textbook is *McCulloch v. Maryland* (1819).[76] A key issue in this case focused on whether Congress could exercise implied powers, and more specifically, on whether Congress could establish a national bank. In the Court's well-known answer, Marshall asserted that a Constitution should be distinguished from ordinary legal codes and that, framed to endure for longer time periods and even to partake of immortality, a Constitution was designed to present the broad outline of power which could be filled in by the other branches. As long as the bank was not a constitutionally prohibited means to a legitimate end, it fell legally within congressionally authorized powers.[77] In so ruling, the Court effectively opened up wide fields for the exercise of congressional powers.

The so-called switch in time that saved nine[78] represents a similar accommodation to congressional power. The story is now well known, but, prior to Franklin Roosevelt's "court-packing plan," the Court had erected a set of barriers to congressional legislation over social and economic matters under the rubric of "substantive due process."[79] In 1937, the Court effectively reversed course, indicating that it would now give fairly minimal scrutiny to matters of economic regulation, thus sanctioning the interventionist economic policies heralded by the New Deal.

In analyzing constitutional amendments, it was clear that there is not always a clear line between sanctioning change and initiating it. The same is true of Supreme Court decisions. Some of the loudest protests from the bench have come when the Court reversed its own precedents to sanction changes initiated by the other branches. Thus, prior to the Court's switch in 1937, citing the economic crisis the states and the nation faced, it had effectively watered down earlier precedents on the contract clause to sanction the Minnesota Mortgage Moratorium Law which provided relief for debtors. Justice Sutherland, one of the so-called conservative Four Horsemen, would have none of this. Stating his view that the written Constitution was unchanging, he said:

> What a court is to do, therefore, is *to declare the law as written*, leaving it to the people themselves to make such changes as new circumstances may require. The meaning of the constitution is fixed when it is adopted, and it is not different at any subsequent time when a court has occasion to pass upon it.[80]

Taking an almost identical position in *West Coast Hotel v. Parrish* (1937), where the Court upheld minimum wage laws despite its earlier decision (written by Sutherland) in *Adkins v. Children's Hospital* (1923),[81] Sutherland said:

The judicial function is that of interpretation; it does not include the power of amendment under the guise of interpretation. To miss the point of difference between the two is to miss all that the phrase "supreme law of the land" stands for and to convert what was intended as inescapable and enduring mandates into mere moral reflections.[82]

For all of its rhetorical power, Sutherland's position is somewhat undermined by the fact that most of the distinctions that he and other conservative justices had devised, for example, the dichotomy between "the heart of the contract" and "mere incidents of employment,"[83] were themselves constitutional encrustations not mandated by the text of the Constitution.[84]

In subsequent decisions, the Court reiterated its earlier renunciations of substantive due process over state and federal economic regulations,[85] while, however, carving out a new niche in the area of protection of personal rights and liberties.[86] Bruce Ackerman is among those who argue that this change was substantive enough to be regarded as one of three important "constitutional moments" in American history.[87]

COURT DECISIONS INITIATING CHANGE

While there is truth in the observation that the Supreme Court is not self-starting and must therefore wait for cases to come to it before it can act, it is clear that over time courts can initiate substantial change by the decisions they render. As in the case of constitutional amendments, there is often a fine line between judicial decisions which initiate change and those which reverse it. Given the potentially far-reaching scope of the Fourteenth Amendment, the previously cited *Brown v. Board of Education* is certainly an example. There are numerous other examples where, much like common law courts in Great Britain, the Courts interstitially fill in gaps in the law.[88]

There are occasions, however, where the Court takes a giant step into uncharted territory, guided less by gaps in the constitutional text than by principles that justices think are or should be embodied there. Undoubtedly, every political scientist and legal scholar has a favorite example. Certainly, however, most commentators agree that the Court went far beyond the explicit commands of the Constitution in enforcing its vision of laissez-faire economics and substantive due process prior to "the switch in time that saved nine."

More recently, some scholars have charged that the Court has reinvented the notion of substantive due process and applied it to the area of privacy.[89] In *Griswold v. Connecticut* (1965), the bellwether decision in this area, Justice Douglas implicated a right of privacy in the penumbras of the First, Third, Fourth, Fifth, Ninth, and Fourteenth Amendments without therefore having to designate which was to carry the weight of the load.[90] Now it was Justice Black's turn to complain that in seeking to read a right of privacy into the Constitution the Court was improperly initiating change:

> For myself, I must with all deference reject that philosophy. The Constitution makers knew the need for change and provided for it. Amendments suggested by the people's elected representatives can be submitted to the people or their selected agents for ratification. That method of change was good for our Fathers, and being somewhat old-fashioned I must add it is good enough for me.[91]

Not only did Justice Black's initial plea fall on seemingly deaf judicial ears, but the Court significantly extended the right to privacy precedent when, over the lonely dissents of Justice White and Rehnquist, in *Roe v. Wade* it declared that the right of privacy was broad enough to encompass this decision.[92] A narrow Court majority finally reached at least a temporary stopping point in *Bowers v. Hardwick* (1986), however, when it refused to declare a Georgia antisodomy law to be unconstitutional. Now speaking for the Court, Justice White pointed to the special dangers of going too far beyond the written constitutional text:

> Nor are we inclined to take a more expansive view of our authority to discover new fundamental rights imbedded in the Due Process Clause. The Court is most vulnerable and comes nearest to illegitimacy when it deals with judge-made constitutional law having little or no cognizable roots in the language or design of the Constitution. . . . There should be, therefore, great resistance to expand the substantive reach of those Clauses, particularly if it requires redefining the category of rights deemed to be fundamental. Otherwise, the Judiciary necessarily takes to itself further authority to govern the country without express constitutional authority. The claimed right pressed on us today falls far short of overcoming this resistance.[93]

White's dictum makes it clear that there are special challenges and problems when the Court seeks to initiate changes on its own without first getting direction from the constitutional text or the actions of the other two branches.

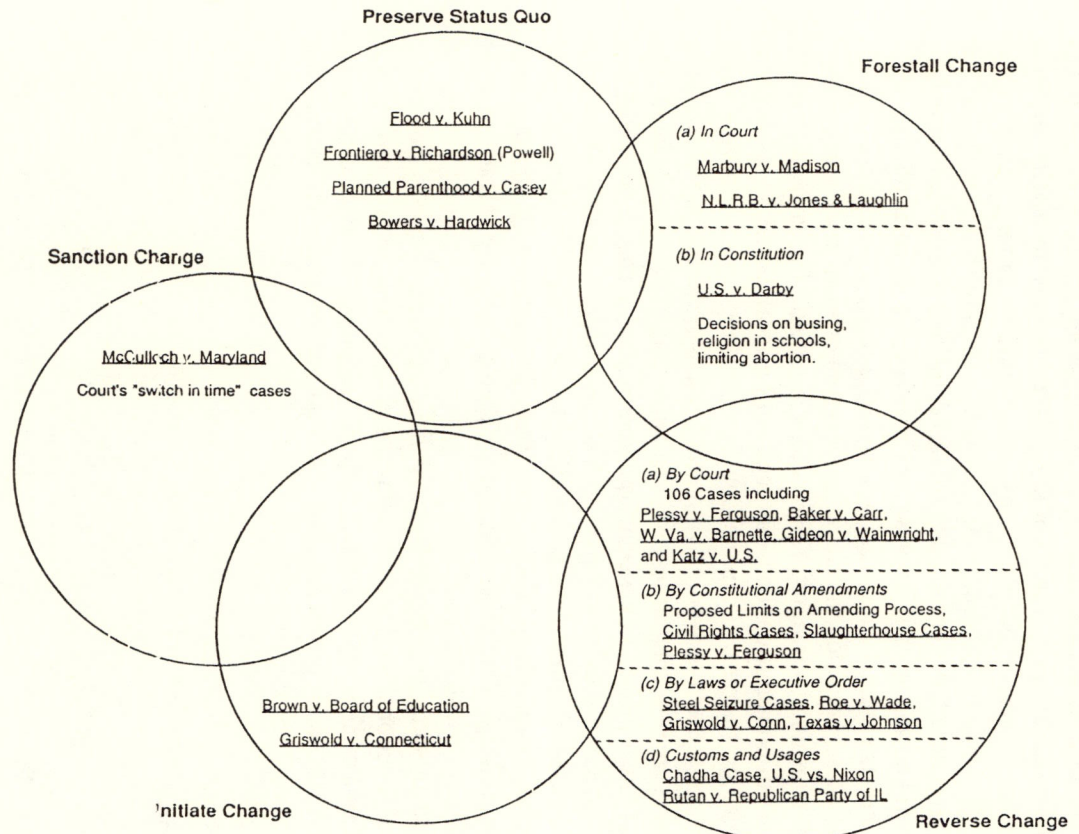

Figure 3.2
Supreme Court Decisions

ANALYSIS

As in the previous chapter, the author has prepared a diagram illustrating the various relationships to change that various examples of judicial review perform. In looking at Figure 3.2, however, it is necessary to return to the caveat at the beginning of this chapter, namely, the recognition that there are so many court decisions spread out over so long a time period that there is little guarantee that any subset of cases like that chosen for this chapter will be representative. Indeed, the best-known cases might be so well known precisely because they appear to be so extraordinary.

Thus, as Figure 3.2 reveals, this chapter has devoted considerable attention to cases in which the Court has reversed or modified changes either by overturning its own prior precedents, by modifying or restricting the impact of constitutional amendments, or by invalidating laws, order, or developing customs. Given the Court's normal deference to *stare decisis*, however, the author would hypothesize that judicial decisions reversing changes are probably far less representative than those cases in which the Court either preserves the status quo or sanctions a change which has already been initiated by one or both of the elected branches. Similarly, while cases initiating changes are fairly dramatic, such changes tend to be associated with special eras (e.g., the Warren Court) or with special issues (e.g., civil rights and liberties) and are therefore hardly characteristic of the Court's usual agenda.

Like the process of amendment, judicial decisions thus perform a variety of functions. Whereas amendments have as their central purpose the initiation of change, the central purposes of judicial decisions would appear to be either preserving the status quo or following the lead of the other branches of government.

NOTES

1. Donald S. Lutz has thus distinguished between the process of "amendment" effected through Article V and the processes of "revision" which are initiated by the legislative and judicial branches. See "Toward a Theory of Constitutional Amendment," paper presented at the American Political Science Convention, Chicago, Illinois, September, 1992, p. 6.

2. Because of its focus on the national government, this book will not address reactions to changes effected through state constitutional provisions, but obviously one reaction to the Supreme Court's perceived restriction of individual rights has been to look to state constitutional provisions for protections that the

national courts no longer provide. See especially William J. Brennan, Jr., "State Constitutions and the Protection of Individual Rights," *Harvard Law Review* 90 (January 1977), pp. 489–504.

3. Walter F. Murphy and C. Herman Pritchett, *Courts, Judges, and Politics: An Introduction to the Judicial Process*, 4th ed. (New York: Random House, 1986), p. 4.

4. Henry J. Abraham, *The Judicial Process*, 6th ed. (New York: Oxford University Press, 1993), p. 272 covers the period through 1992.

5. 407 U.S. 258 (1972).

6. 411 U.S. 677, 792 (1973).

7. 112 S. Ct. 2791 (1992). For a similar discussion of *stare decisis* in the context of abortion, see Justice Powell's opinion in *City of Akron v. Akron Center for Reproductive Health* 462 U.S. 416 (1983).

8. 410 U.S. 113 (1973). This case and its historical antecedents are discussed in great detail in David J. Garrow, *Liberty and Sexuality: The Right to Privacy and the Making of Roe v. Wade* (New York: Macmillan, 1994).

9. For an account of the numerous changes that the Court did accept in this area, see Lee Epstein and Joseph F. Kobylka, *The Supreme Court and Legal Change: Abortion and the Death Penalty* (Chapel Hill: University of North Carolina Press, 1992).

10. The Court's *dicta* on *stare decisis* in Casey are criticized in Michael S. Paulsen, review of *The Constitution in Conflict*, *Constitutional Commentary* 10 (Winter 1993), pp. 225–33 and in Eugene W. Hickok and Gary L. McDowell, *Justice vs. Law: Courts and Politics in American Society* (New York: The Free Press, 1993), pp. 169–90. For a critique which is more sympathetic to the view of *stare decisis* defended in that case by O'Connor, Kennedy, and Souter, see Michael J. Gerhardt, "The Pressure of Precedent: A Critique of the Conservative Approaches to Stare Decisis in Abortion Cases," *Constitutional Commentary* 10 (Winter 1993), pp. 67–86.

11. *Planned Parenthood v. Casey*, 112 S. Ct. 2791, 2808 (1992).

12. Ibid., p. 2809. In an article focusing on judicial precedent, Geoffrey R. Stone cites three major occasions when precedents should be overridden—when based on factual error, when "premised on a state of affairs that has changed so much over time that the Justices who reached the prior decision would themselves have reached a different result in light of the changed circumstances," and when justices "conclude that a prior decision was simply 'wrong' at the time it was decided." See "Precedent, the Amendment Process, and Evolution in Constitutional Doctrine," *Harvard Journal of Law & Public Policy* 11 (Winter 1988), p. 71. Stones argues that the third reason is the most "problematic."

13. 300 U.S. 379 (1937).

14. 347 U.S. 483 (1954).

15. *Planned Parenthood v. Casey*, 112 S. Ct. 2814 (1992).

16. Ibid.

17. Ibid., p. 2815.

18. Ibid.

19. For details of this controversy, see William H. Rehnquist, *Grand Inquests: The Historic Impeachments of Justice Samuel Chase and President Andrew Johnson* (New York: William Morrow, 1992).

20. *Marbury v. Madison,* 1 Cranch (5 U.S.) 137 (1803).

21. 301 U.S. 1 (1937).

22. See William E. Leuchenburg, "The Origins of Franklin D. Roosevelt's 'Court-Packing' Plan," *Supreme Court Review,* ed. Philip Kurland (Chicago: University of Chicago Press, 1966), pp. 347–400.

23. At his first meeting with the other justices, Justice Taft is reputed to have said, "I was put on this Court to reverse some of the decisions you people have been making." Quoted in Arthur S. Miller, "Lord Chancellor, Warren Earl Burger," *Society* 10 (March/April 1973), p. 18.

24. See Henry J. Abraham, *Justices and Presidents: A Political History of Appointments to the Supreme Court,* 3d ed. (New York: Oxford University Press, 1992), p. 14.

25. *United States v. Darby Lumber Co.,* 312 U.S. 100 (1941).

26. 354 U.S. 1 (1957).

27. See Duane Tananbaum, *The Bricker Amendment Controversy: A Test of Eisenhower's Political Leadership* (Ithaca, NY: Cornell University Press, 1988).

28. See, for example, *Milliken v. Bradley,* 418 U.S. 717 (1974).

29. *Board of Education of the Westside Community Schools v. Mergens,* 496 U.S. 226 (1990).

30. See, for example, *Webster v. Reproductive Health Services,* 492 U.S. 490 (1989).

31. Morris L. Ernst, *The Great Reversals: Tales of the Supreme Court* (New York: Weybright and Talley, 1973).

32. For the role of such dissents in constitutional development, see Donald E. Lively, *Foreshadows of the Law: Supreme Court Dissents and Constitutional Development* (Westport, CT: Praeger, 1992).

33. Ernst, *The Great Reversals,* p. 1, p. 12.

34. See appendix to Michael J. Gerhardt, "The Role of Precedent in Constitutional Decisionmaking and Theory," *The George Washington Law Review* 60 (November 1991), pp. 147–59.

35. Thus, Clement Vose, who has written one of the most comprehensive treatments of the relationship between judicial review and constitutional amendment, identifies "the process by which the United States Supreme Court has overruled the Court's previous decisions" as "the most distinctive and dramatic technique of constitutional change in this century." See *Constitutional Change: Amendment Politics and Supreme Court Litigation Since 1900* (Lexington, MA: Lexington Books, 1972), p. xxiii.

36. 347 U.S. 483 (1954).

37. 163 U.S. 537 (1896).

38. It should be noted that the decision in *Brown v. Board of Education* followed extensive litigation, particularly by the NAACP Legal Defense Fund, over a twenty- to thirty-year period. See Richard Kluger, *Simple Justice*, 2 vols. (New York: Alfred A. Knopf, 1975).

Michael J. Klarman, "*Brown*, Racial Change, and the Civil Rights Movement," *Virginia Law Review* 80 (February 1994), pp. 7–150, presents the view that most changes in civil rights policies would have occurred without the *Brown v. Board of Education* decision. Klarman further argues that the influence of *Brown* was more indirect than direct in that its primary significance lay in the political opposition and acts of violence that it spawned, actions which riveted national attention on civil rights issues. However this specific thesis is ultimately judged, it certainly calls attention to the fact that, in constitutional law, lines of causation may sometimes be more indirect than direct. Klarman's analysis also lends some further plausibility to the arguments of Gerald N. Rosenberg—addressed in the "efficacy" section in the last chapter of this book—which question the effectiveness of attempts by the Supreme Court to effect social change. For Rosenberg's comments on Klarman's article, see "*Brown* is Dead! Long Live *Brown*!: The Endless Attempt to Canonize a Case," *Virginia Law Review* 80 (February 1994), pp. 161–72.

39. 369 U.S. 186 (1962).

40. 328 U.S. 549 (1946). This case was, however, a four-to-three decision with Justice Stone's seat vacant and Justice Frankfurter not participating.

41. 319 U.S. 624 (1943).

42. 310 U.S. 586 (1940). The reversal occurred through a combination of new membership on the Court (Stone being elevated to the place occupied by Chief Justice Hughes and Jackson and Rutledge replacing Stone and McReynolds) and by a change of heart on the parts of Justices Douglas, Black, and Murphy. See Gerhardt, "The Role of Precedent," p. 99.

43. 389 U.S. 347 (1967).

44. 277 U.S. 438 (1928).

45. 372 U.S. 335 (1963).

46. 316 U.S. 455 (1942).

47. 111 S. Ct. 2597 (1991).

48. 482 U.S. 496 (1987).

49. 490 U.S. 805 (1989).

50. Dennis J. Horan, Edward R. Grant, and Paige C. Cunningham, eds., *Abortion and the Constitution: Reversing Roe v. Wade Through the Courts* (Washington, DC: Georgetown University Press, 1987), p. xi.

51. These arguments are reviewed in John R. Vile, *Contemporary Questions Surrounding the Constitutional Amending Process* (Westport, CT: Praeger, 1993), pp. 127–54.

52. These arguments were applied to the Fifteenth, Eighteenth, and Nineteenth Amendments. For these arguments, see John R. Vile, *The Constitutional Amending Process in American Political Thought* (New York: Praeger, 1992), pp. 157–82.

53. See, for example, *The National Prohibition Cases*, 253 U.S. 350 (1920) and *Leser v. Garnett*, 258 U.S. 130 (1922).

54. These cross-purposes are ably described in William E. Nelson, *The Fourteenth Amendment: From Political Principle to Judicial Doctrine* (Cambridge, MA: Harvard University Press, 1988).

55. 83 U.S. 36, p. 78. State courts sometimes used similar arguments in attempting to contain the scope of the Nineteenth Amendment granting women's suffrage. See Jennifer K. Brown, "The Nineteenth Amendment and Women's Equality," *The Yale Law Journal* 102 (June 1993), p. 2196.

56. 109 U.S. 3 (1883).

57. 163 U.S. 537 (1896).

58. Cass R. Sunstein cites *Plessy v. Ferguson*, ibid., along with *Lochner v. New York*, 198 U.S. 45 (1905) and *Muller v. Oregon*, 208 U.S. 412 (1908) as examples of when the Court "took existing practice as the baseline for deciding issues of neutrality and partisanship." In his judgment, Plessy thus serves as an example of the Supreme Court upholding the status quo. See *The Partial Constitution* (Cambridge, MA: Harvard University Press, 1993), p. 41.

59. 453 U.S. 57 (1981), p. 64.

60. Abraham, *The Judicial Process*, p. 272.

61. Ibid.

62. 247 U.S. 251 (1918).

63. 259 U.S. 20 (1922).

64. For further analysis beginning with congressional attempts to pass legislation and ending with attempts to adopt an amendment and the Court's eventual repudiation of its initial decisions, see Mark E. Herrmann, "Looking Down from the Hill: Factors Determining the Success of Congressional Efforts to Reverse Supreme Court Interpretations of the Constitution," *William and Mary Law Review* 33 (Winter 1992), pp. 547–68.

65. *Youngstown Sheet & Tube Co. v. Sawyer*, 343 U.S. 579 (1952).

66. 381 U.S. 479 (1965).

67. 410 U.S. 113 (1973).

68. 491 U.S. 397 (1989).

69. 496 U.S. 310 (1990).

70. Robert F. Nagel cites, for example, judicial acquiescence in congressional judgments regarding such matters as "the definition of a quorum for purposes of enacting legislation, the number of votes required to override a veto, the formalities of the presidential signature, and the intricacies of the use of the veto power." See *Constitutional Cultures: The Mentality and Consequences of Judicial Review* (Berkeley: University of California Press, 1989), p. 14.

71. *Immigration and Naturalization Service v. Chadha*, 462 U.S. 919 (1983).

72. 418 U.S. 683 (1974).

73. On jury size, see *Williams v. Florida*, 399 U.S. 78 (1970). On jury unanimity, see *Johnson v. Louisiana*, 406 U.S. 356 (1972) and *Apodaca v. Oregon*, 406 U.S. 404 (1972).

74. 110 S. Ct. 2719 (1990). Also see *Elrod v. Burns*, 427 U.S. 347 (1976) and *Branti v. Finkel*, 445 U.S. 507 (1980).

75. Alexander M. Bickel, *The Least Dangerous Branch: The Supreme Court at the Bar of Politics*, 2d ed. (New Haven, CT: Yale University Press, 1986), pp. 29–33.

76. 4 Wheat (17 U.S.) 316 (1819).

77. Ibid., p. 321. Marshall thus argued: "Let the end be legitimate, let it be within the scope of the constitution, and all means which are appropriate, which are plainly adapted to that end, which are not prohibited, but consist with the letter and spirit of the constitution, are constitutional."

78. See *West Coast Hotel v. Parrish*, 300 U.S. 379 (1937) and *National Labor Relations Board v. Jones & Laughlin Steel Corp.*, 301 U.S. 1 (1937).

79. These developments are often tied to *Lochner v. New York*, 198 U.S. 45 (1905), which epitomized the Court's stance. For a discussion of the logic behind substantive due process, see Howard Gillman, *The Constitution Besieged: The Rise and Demise of Lochner Era Police Powers Jurisdiction* (Durham, NC: Duke University Press, 1993).

80. *Home Building and Loan Association v. Blaisdell*, 290 U.S. 398, 451 (1934).

81. 261 U.S. 525 (1923).

82. *West Coast Hotel v. Parrish*, 300 U.S. 379, p. 404.

83. Alpheus T. Mason, *The Supreme Court from Taft to Burger*, 3d ed. (Baton Rouge: Louisiana State University Press, 1979), p. 62.

84. Hickok and McDowell, *Justice vs. Law*, p. 112.

85. See, for example, *Williamson v. Lee Optical Company*, 348 U.S. 483 (1955) and *Ferguson v. Skrupa*, 372 U.S. 726 (1973).

86. See Justice Stone's famous footnote four in *United States v. Carolene Products Company*, 304 U.S. 144 (1938).

87. Ackerman, *We the People*.

88. Benjamin Cardozo, *The Nature of the Judicial Process* (New Haven, CT: Yale University Press, 1949), pp. 14–18.

89. For such a critique, see Wallace Mendleson, "Sex and the Singular Constitution: What Remains of *Roe v. Wade*?" *PS: Political Science & Politics* 26 (June 1993), pp. 206–08.

90. 381 U.S. 479, 484–85 (1965).

91. 381 U.S. 479, p. 522. Also see Hugo L. Black, *A Constitutional Faith* (New York: Alfred A. Knopf, 1969), p. 21. Black took a similar stance when, in *Harper v. Virginia Board of Elections*, the Court utilized the notion of an evolving Constitution to strike down state poll taxes. See 383 U.S. 663, 676 (1966).

92. 410 U.S. 113 (1973). Significantly, the Court's decision followed the liberalization of abortion laws in a number of states. See Gerald N. Rosenberg, *The Hollow Hope: Can Courts Bring About Social Change?* (Chicago: University of Chicago Press, 1991), pp. 178–79.

93. *Bowers v. Hardwick*, 478 U.S. 186 (1986), pp. 194–95.

Chapter 4

A Selective Look at the Impact of the Political Branches in Effecting Change

Although scholars sometimes describe constitutional amendments and judicial decisions as the real dynamos of change within society, in terms of sheer volume, the legislative and executive branches undoubtedly initiate most changes at both the state and national level. Given the importance of elections and electoral accountability in the American political system, this is certainly consistent with democratic theory. Politicians typically run for office promising to initiate reforms, and voters see their elections as evidence that the majority favor their proposals. Especially in landslide and in so-called critical, or realigning, elections, politicians may come into office with a strong mandate for change.[1]

Laws and executive orders, like constitutional amendments and judicial decisions, can be located on a line in terms of their relationship to change, as demonstrated in Figure 4.1.

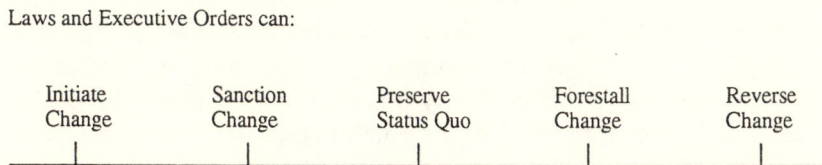

Laws and Executive Orders can:

Initiate Change	Sanction Change	Preserve Status Quo	Forestall Change	Reverse Change

Figure 4.1
Laws and Executive Orders and Change

SPECIAL PROBLEMS IN ANALYZING CHANGES BY THE ELECTED BRANCHES

Three problems complicate the discussion of legislation and executive orders. First, given the malleability of the U.S. Constitution and the fact that it is surrounded by a much wider "constitution," there is no ready way to distinguish those laws and orders which deal with "constitutional" concerns and those which do not.[2] Second, absent a doctrine of parliamentary sovereignty such as that which is in place in Great Britain,[3] there are obvious limits to legislative and executive tinkering with the Constitution. Thus, there is an ever-present possibility that the courts will invalidate legislative and executive attempts to initiate change. Third, as in the discussion of judicial decisions, there are so many laws and orders covering such a long time period that it is difficult to know whether any sample is representative. As with the previous examination of judicial decisions, then, this chapter will focus less on seeking a representative sample than in identifying laws and executive orders which fulfill each of the five functions identified above.

A NOTE ON THE APPOINTMENT AND CONFIRMATION PROCESS

Before looking at laws and executive orders which exemplify various postures toward change, it bears noting that a major vehicle whereby the political branches influence constitutional change is the process of appointing and confirming heads of government agencies, and, especially, members of the judicial branch. Any examination of the history of presidential appointments to the bench will demonstrate that this is a highly political process.[4] Moreover, not only do presidents sometimes fail to get their choices approved by the Senate (especially at the Supreme Court where approximately one of four nominees is rejected),[5] but many have also been sadly disappointed by their nominees.[6] This author will not further pursue the impact of the appointment and confirmation processes in this book. By this decision, he does not mean to disparage the appointment and confirmation processes but rather to recognize that these processes eventually result in changes that are subsumed under the rubric of the judicial capacity for change discussed in the previous chapter.

LIMITS ON THE POLITICAL PROCESSES

In a constitutional system, presidential authority is necessarily limited. Executive orders generally extend only to areas where Congress delegates authority to the president, especially over military affairs—where executive agreements with foreign countries fulfill a function similar to congressionally approved treaties[7]—or to areas involving control over members or policies of the executive branch. Since 1907 (when executive orders began to be numbered), presidents have issued over 15,000 of them.[8]

Laws are undoubtedly even more numerous. A number of features of the constitutional system, including federalism, bicameralism, and the separation of powers, complicate the processes of lawmaking in the United States. Some observers have thus noted what they call "the tyranny of the status quo" within this political system.[9] The principle of federalism leads to perpetual dialogue, and sometimes conflict, as to the appropriate division of power between state and national authorities.[10] Bicameralism arguably delays, and possibly refines, laws by requiring that they do not become effective until adopted in identical form by both houses of Congress.[11] Separation of powers assures that the will of Congress is subject to modification both by the threat of executive veto and by the possibility that laws Congress passes will subsequently be declared unconstitutional by the courts. In addition to these constitutionally mandated obstacles to hasty reform, internal changes in the 1970s which led to the further dispersion of power within Congress among a host of committees, subcommittees, and their chairs have arguably complicated the lawmaking process even beyond what the American Framers may have intended.[12]

LAWS AND EXECUTIVE ORDERS DESIGNED TO PRESERVE THE STATUS QUO

The first several months of the Clinton administration provide a good example of some of the interdepartmental conflict that can be generated when the executive and legislative branches have different conceptions of the public good. Clinton assumed office with the announced intention of overturning a 1992 military statute banning gays in the U.S. military. Yet almost immediately he ran into conflict when leading Senators and other members of Congress announced that if the president initiated his plans through executive order without any compromise, they would overturn this order through legislation. Congress held a series of hearings on the subject, and those hearings as well as public reaction eventually forced the president to compromise his position.[13] Similarly, Congress reacted negatively to President Clinton's announced intention of lifting the ban on preventing immigrants from residing in the United States if they had the AIDS virus.[14] Clearly, while the president viewed himself as an agent of change, important members of Congress saw themselves as preservers of the status quo.

President Clinton had also promised to protect the rights of American women to obtain legal abortions, a sentiment possibly favored by a majority of both houses of Congress. One vehicle for preserving this right is the proposed Freedom of Choice Act which would in effect sanction existing court decisions which nationalize the right to an abortion.[15] Thus, Dawn Johnsen, an attorney with the National Abortion Rights Action League, described the act as codifying "the case law from 1973 to 1988."[16] At least one commentator has noted the problematic nature of such legislation:

> When Congress seeks to preserve constitutional law that the Court is trying to erase, the political and constitutional burdens on Congress are acute. In such a context, statutory interpretation may be "dynamic" in a backward-looking sense. Even as Congress endeavors to restore or preserve, the entity charged with responsibility for construing its instructions may be trying to limit or destroy. One cannot be sanguine about the results of a broad delegation to such an entity.[17]

This and other concerns help account for the Congress's failure to act on the law during the first year of the Clinton administration.[18]

LAWS AND EXECUTIVE ORDERS DESIGNED TO FORESTALL CHANGE

While the congressional attempt to prevent President Clinton from opening the U.S. military to gays is an example of attempting to preserve the status quo, it also serves the purpose of illustrating how Congress may use laws to forestall changes contemplated by other branches of the government. To the extent that proposed national laws supporting the right to an abortion are designed to forestall more conservative decisions by the Supreme Court, they have much the same motivation.

The Equal Access Act of 1984 may be interpreted in similar fashion. Faced with a number of judicial decisions limiting religious exercises in public schools,[19] Congress saw an apparent opening in a decision permitting religious organizations to meet on college campuses that provided an open public forum.[20] In a decision subsequently upheld by the Supreme Court,[21] Congress subsequently extended similar protections to clubs meeting on high school campuses.[22]

LAWS AND EXECUTIVE ORDERS DESIGNED TO REVERSE CHANGE

As in the case of changes initiated by judicial decisions, laws and executive orders may be designed to reverse changes in a number of ways. Laws and executive orders may thus repeal earlier laws or executive actions, overturn or modify judicial constructions of prior laws, or overturn or modify customs and usages which have not been formally frozen into law.

Laws and Orders Designed to Repeal or Modify Earlier Laws and Orders

The Clinton administration again provides an instance of a president committed to reverse executive orders initiated by a previous president. Two examples stand out particularly. In one instance, President Clinton reversed a gag order which Presidents Reagan and Bush had issued on abortion counseling[23] and which the Supreme Court had subsequently upheld, although certainly not mandated.[24] Clinton also reversed an earlier presidential order banning fetal tissue research.[25]

On the legislative front, in what is generally considered to be the first realigning election in American history, Thomas Jefferson came into office with what he considered to be a clear mandate to reverse Federalist policies. Fortunately, Republicans in the U.S. House had already added a termination date to the Sedition Act of 1798 which Jefferson had so detested.[26] Still on the books, however, was the Judiciary Act of 1801 (actually adopted by a lame-duck Federalist majority after Jefferson was elected president) which was intended to ensconce Federalists in the judicial branch. This act abolished existing circuits (along with the much-detested duty of Supreme Court justices to ride circuit), created new ones, widened federal judicial jurisdiction, and reduced the number of Supreme Court justices from six members to five, effective with the next vacancy. Not only did the incoming Republicans repeal the law, but, seeking to stave off judicial invalidation of their work, in the Judiciary Act of 1802, they also postponed the next session of the U.S. Supreme Court until February of the following year.[27]

A more current law that could meet a similar fate is the so-called Hyde Amendment which seriously limits federal Medicaid funding of abortion and which has been upheld by the Supreme Court.[28] Although he has not, as of this writing, mustered the necessary majorities to repeal this law,[29] the Hyde Amendment stands in direct opposition to Clinton's announced stance on this issue. This issue is likely to prove important in the context of any proposed national health care plan.

The constitutional obstacles to quick passage of legislation have already been noted. These obstacles serve to reduce the occasions when policies oscillate widely from one administration to another, even when these administrations represent differing political parties.[30] They also cut down on the number of laws adopted to repeal others.

Not surprisingly, perhaps, presidents especially often find it easier to change policies through use of their appointment power and through executive orders rather than through seeking repeal of legislation. Thus, although President Ronald Reagan announced that he opposed having a cabinet-level Secretary of Education,[31] he subsequently filled this position with a strong partisan of his own policies. Similarly, Reagan made cutbacks in personnel in the Environmental Protection Agency and in the Department of the Interior and appointed leaders whose hostility to the agencies' missions made it more difficult for these agencies to carry out the regulatory policies that Reagan opposed.[32] It is almost a truism that Presidents, while not always successful, seek to fill the federal judiciary with individuals compatible with their own philosophies.[33]

Laws and Orders Designed to Overturn Court Decisions

Scholars commonly distinguish between judicial decisions which are based on constitutional interpretation and those which are based simply on statutory construction. In theory, at least, only an amendment or another judicial decision can reverse a judicial decision based on constitutional grounds, whereas new laws may reverse court decisions based simply on statutory interpretation.[34] The line between these two areas is not, however, always so clear,[35] and, to this author's knowledge, no one has systematically compiled the number of times that Congress has reversed judicial decisions,[36] meaning that any descriptions of such events must be fairly episodic.

Thus, in 1981 and 1982, some members of Congress pushed actively for the Helms' Human Life Statute which sought to overturn the effects of *Roe v. Wade*[37] by affirmatively answering the question—whether or not human life begins at conception—that the Court had attempted to sidestep. Apparently, questions about the constitutionality of this law were among the factors motivating many members of Congress to give greater attention to the Hatch Human Life Federalism Amendment.[38] This would not be the only time, however, that members of Congress contemplated or adopted legislation in an attempt to overturn or modify court decisions.

Thus, when faced with a decision by the Supreme Court invalidating a Texas flag-desecration law as a violation of the free speech rights outlined in the First Amendment,[39] Congress enacted an alternate federal law, the 1989 Flag Protection Act, to accomplish this same object.[40] While this law gave a narrowly divided Court a quick opportunity to reconsider a very controversial decision, the law was not ultimately successful in accomplishing its professed purpose, and, absent a constitutional amendment, the Court's decision stands as law of the land.[41]

Congress was more successful in outlawing discrimination in places of public accommodation through the Civil Rights Act of 1964. Eighty-one years before, the Court had invalidated a similar law—the Civil Rights Act of 1875—on the basis that Congress did not have authority under the Fourteenth Amendment to prohibit discriminatory private (in contrast to state) action.[42] After considerable deliberation, Congress evaded or bypassed this precedent by predicating its authority in the 1964 Civil Rights Act on its power over interstate commerce,[43] and the Supreme Court subsequently validated the law in *Heart of Atlanta Motel v. United States* (1964)[44] and *Katzenbach v. McClung* (1964).[45] The adoption of the Religious Freedom Restoration Act,[46] whose central intention is to restore judicial interpretations of the free exercise clause prior to the Supreme Court's decision in *Employment Division v. Smith* (1990),[47] represents another attempt to reverse a change or a perceived change in judicial interpretation.

A more typical case[48] involving an attempt by the Congress to clarify existing law was actually initiated by a Supreme Court decision in *United States v. South-Eastern Underwriters Association* (1944).[49] Overturning long-standing precedents initiated by *Paul v. Virginia* (1869),[50] a plurality of the Court decided that insurance companies doing substantial business within different states were involved in interstate commerce and could thus be regulated by the federal government. In the McCarran Act of 1945, Congress subsequently indicated that it wanted regulation to rest, as in the past, with the states.

Similarly, although the Supreme Court declared that employers were not required to provide disability payments for pregnant workers,[51] Congress later amended the Civil Rights Act of 1964 to mandate such coverage.[52] When the Supreme Court declared that public transit was subject to the minimum wage and overtime requirements of the Fair Labor Standards Act,[53]

Congress amended this law.[54] When the Supreme Court upheld a military regulation forbidding a member of the U.S. Air Force from wearing a yarmulke while on duty,[55] Congress amended a military authorization bill to reverse this judgment.[56] Likewise, when the Supreme Court modified earlier disparate impact decisions[57] in *Wards Cove Packing Co. v. Atonio* (1989),[58] Congress responded by adopting the Civil Rights Act of 1991 which attempted to restore application of more forceful standards. Apparently, there is still considerable ambiguity about the application of that law.[59]

Laws and Orders Designed to Change Existing Customs and Usages

Political parties have grown within the silences of the Constitution, and, along with parties came attempts to staff the government with partisans favorable to the party in power. While the Constitution continues to permit considerable discretion, especially in top-level cabinet and judicial decisions, one major legislative endeavor in the nineteenth century was the attempt to reduce the perceived evils of the so-called spoils system by creating a Civil Service Commission.[60] In making employment conditional upon perceptions of achievement and objective merit rather than political acceptability, Congress modified a custom that had grown without specific constitutional sanction.

One could interpret the Budget and Impoundment Act of 1974 in a similar light. Presidents as far back as Thomas Jefferson had utilized some impoundment powers, especially in cases where money that had been appropriated (for defense, for example) no longer seemed needed, but President Nixon significantly expanded use of the authority, refusing, for example, to spend money under the revised Federal Water Pollution Act of 1972 even after Congress overrode his veto on the subject.[61] Congress subsequently adopted the Budget and Impoundment Act of 1974 distinguishing deferrals from outright rescissions and generally proving far more willing to accept the former than the latter.[62]

Congress also introduced the War Powers Resolution of 1973 as a way of restoring the *status quo ante*, after criticism increased during the Korean and Vietnam conflicts that American presidents were taking unilateral actions in foreign affairs without proper consultation with and approval from Congress. The law requires presidential consultation and notification and limits the commitment of troops abroad to sixty days (with a possible thirty day extension), absent congressional approval. Significantly, Congress specifically denied that the law was designed to alter the powers of the two elected branches as specified in the Constitution.[63]

In part because the act contains a legislative veto mechanism which was declared unconstitutional in a case involving another law,[64] and in part because the law deals with areas in which courts generally defer judgments,[65] the War Powers Resolution does not appear to have proven to be particularly successful, but it still stands as a symbol of the congressional determination to put some restraints on presidential war powers and may, in the words of one astute observer, "condition interbranch negotiation."[66]

The Gramm-Rudman-Hollins Deficit Reduction Act of 1985 is also a law designed to reverse developing custom, in this case that of deficit financing which began to spiral in the 1970s and 1980s.[67] The constitutional dimensions of the law designed to provide automatic budget cuts or "sequesters" in cases where projected deficits did not come within targeted figures were evidenced by the fact that many viewed this bill as an alternative to a Balanced Budget Amendment.[68] Significantly, some of the same problems that have plagued the Gramm-Rudman-Hollings Bill—especially the difficulty of making accurate budget projections and the possibility that deficits may sometimes be necessary and/or desirable—are also problems that many scholars believe would ultimately frustrate a constitutional amendment on the subject.

LAWS AND ORDERS DESIGNED TO SANCTION CHANGE

In above discussions, the possibility of a law designed to protect a woman's constitutional right to an abortion was cited as an example of a law that would preserve the status quo by heading off a possible change of heart by the Court. An alternative way to understand this law, however, would be as a sanction to a change initiated when the federal courts decided that abortion would be a national right. Similarly, when in 1970 Congress attempted through the adoption of amendments to the 1965 Voting Rights Act to extend the right to vote to individuals from eighteen to twenty-one years old, it was in part simply extending a movement to lower the voting age which had already begun in some of the states.[69]

LAWS AND ORDERS DESIGNED TO INITIATE CHANGE

Probably the most common role anticipated for laws and executive orders is that of initiating change. As noted previously in this chapter, this was President Clinton's object when he announced his intention to lift the ban on immigration by those with the HIV virus as well as his intention to reverse existing military policy on acceptance of gays into the armed forces. Indeed, combatting discrimination has been one of three major purposes for which executive orders have been utilized in the postwar period (controlling executive bureaucracies and maintaining secrets are the other two).[70] Thus, Harry Truman issued an executive order in 1948 to integrate the armed services while Lyndon Johnson subsequently used this mechanism to mandate minority hiring by firms doing business with the federal government.[71]

Presidents in this century have demonstrated how the power of their office, combined with a legislation-oriented Congress, can institute real societal change. Probably nothing has yet matched Franklin Roosevelt's first 100 days in office, but certainly Lyndon Johnson's legislative successes after his landslide election of 1964, and to a lesser extent, Reagan's successes with a Congress where one house was still dominated by the party in opposition, demonstrate the kinds and scope of changes that can be initiated through legislative channels.[72] These may involve the creation of new agencies and programs, the reallocation of tax burdens and benefits, the initiation or relaxation of regulatory codes and penalties, and so forth. While not all these actions are strictly "constitutional," many such changes have constitutional ramifications.

One striking possibility that has emerged in recent years is that Congress might have greater authority under the enforcement provisions of the Fourteenth and Fifteenth Amendments to extend individual rights than would the courts acting on their own. Thus, in *Katzenbach v. Morgan*,[73] the Supreme Court cited Section 5 of the Fourteenth Amendment in upholding a provision of the Voting Rights Act of 1965 outlawing application of literacy tests to those who had completed the sixth grade in non-English-speaking schools, despite an earlier decision where the Court had upheld the constitutionality of these tests as against state action alone.[74]

ANALYSIS

Figure 4.2 should show that laws and executive orders clearly cover the entire gamut in instituting and forestalling change, sometimes in cooperation with one another and at other times in conflict.

There is perhaps somewhat less finality in such decisions not simply because subsequent congresses and presidents may reverse them (just as one court might reverse an earlier judicial decision), but also because they

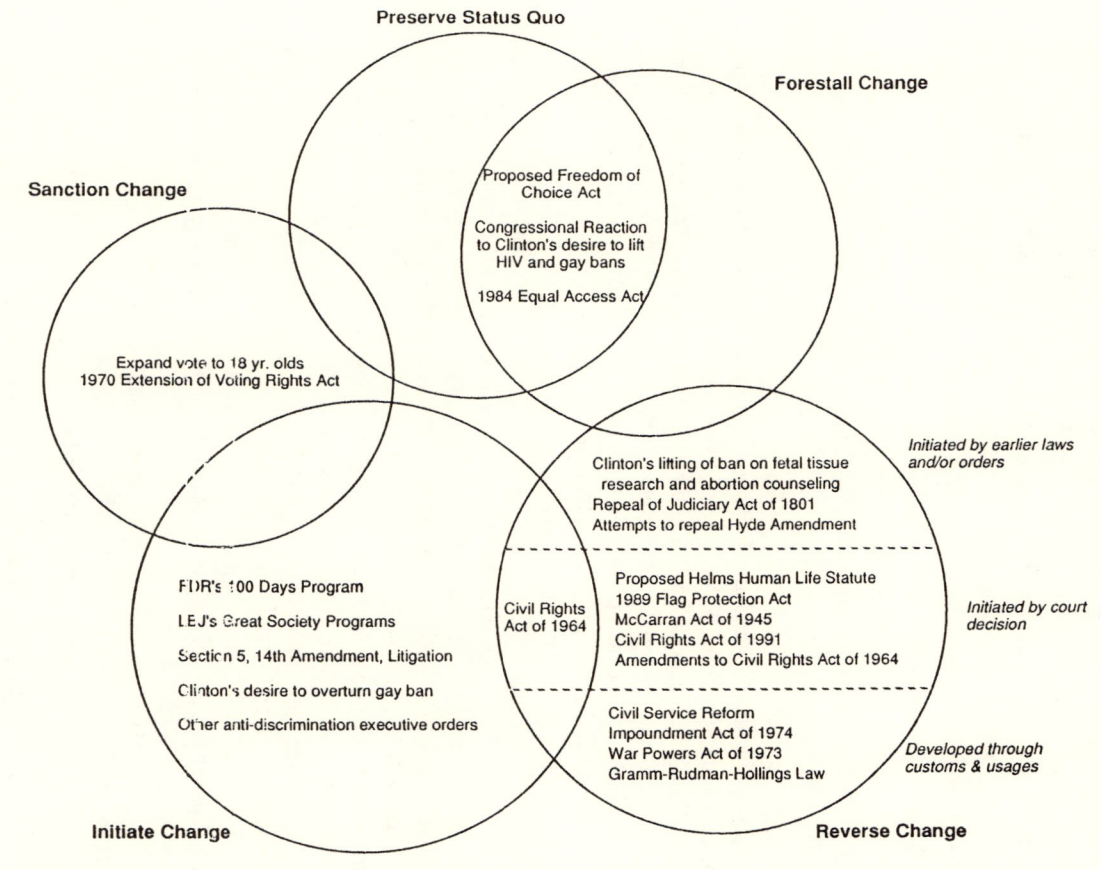

Figure 4.2
Laws and Executive Orders

Preserve Status Quo

Forestall Change

Sanction Change

Proposed Freedom of Choice Act

Congressional Reaction to Clinton's desire to lift HIV and gay bans

1984 Equal Access Act

Expand vote to 18 yr. olds
1970 Extension of Voting Rights Act

Clinton's lifting of ban on fetal tissue research and abortion counseling
Repeal of Judiciary Act of 1801
Attempts to repeal Hyde Amendment

Initiated by earlier laws and/or orders

FDR's 100 Days Program

LBJ's Great Society Programs

Section 5, 14th Amendment, Litigation

Clinton's desire to overturn gay ban

Other anti-discrimination executive orders

Civil Rights Act of 1964

Proposed Helms Human Life Statute
1989 Flag Protection Act
McCarran Act of 1945
Civil Rights Act of 1991
Amendments to Civil Rights Act of 1964

Initiated by court decision

Civil Service Reform
Impoundment Act of 1974
War Powers Act of 1973
Gramm-Rudman-Hollings Law

Developed through customs & usages

Initiate Change

Reverse Change

are subject to judicial review. Hence, the courts have reversed a number of laws examined in this chapter, including many early New Deal programs, the 1970 extension of voting rights to eighteen year olds, and the 1989 Flag Protection Act. Other actions—the proposed Human Life Statute, for example—were either never effected or—as in the case of the War Powers Resolution of 1973 and the Gramm-Rudman-Hollings Act—do not appear to have been altogether successful. Such examples should not, however, obscure the many instances in which the two elected branches have filled in constitutional gaps and contributed to the dynamics of constitutional growth and development.[75]

NOTES

1. See Walter D. Burnham, *Critical Elections and the Mainsprings of American Politics* (New York: W. W. Norton, 1970).

2. In a recent article, Ira C. Lupu refers to what he calls, "statutes revolving in constitutional law orbits." He further divides such statutes into four categories, those which: "1) extend a constitutional concept to a level of government, or to a government entity, to which courts had not previously extended it; 2) extend application of constitutional limits beyond state action to private activity; 3) restore a constitutional concept that courts have abandoned; or 4) respond to an authoritative judicial pronouncement concerning the constitutional boundaries of permissible regulation." See Ira C. Lupu, "Statutes Revolving in Constitutional Law Orbits," *Virginia Law Review* 79 (February 1993), p. 4. Lupu notes that legislation often "tracks" either the language of the Constitution itself or the language of prominent court decisions interpreting the Constitution. He further observes, p. 76, that such statutes "test our prevailing notions of the methods of constitutional change" and especially the view that such changes are initiated either by amendments or by judicial interpretations.

3. See John R. Vile, "Three Kinds of Constitutional Founding and Change: The Convention Model and Its Alternatives," *Political Research Quarterly* (December 1993), pp. 881–95.

4. John Massaro, *Supremely Political* (Albany: State University of New York Press, 1990). Also see Henry J. Abraham, *Justices and Presidents: A Political History of Appointments to the Supreme Court*, 3d ed. (New York: Oxford University Press, 1992).

5. Abraham notes that the Senate has failed to confirm 30 of 143 nominees to the Supreme Court made by the president. See Henry J. Abraham, *The Judicial Process*, 6th ed. (New York: Oxford University Press, 1993), p. 75.

6. Abraham, ibid. p. 74, cites Truman as saying "packing the Supreme Court simply can't be done. I've tried and it won't work. Whenever you put a man on the Supreme Court he ceases to be your friend. I'm sure of that." On the same page,

Abraham cites Teddy Roosevelt—disappointed with a decision rendered by Oliver Wendell Holmes, Jr., in an anti-trust case—as saying, "I could carve out of a banana a Judge with more backbone than that!"

7. Stephen R. Munzer and James W. Nickel, "Does the Constitution Mean What It Always Meant?" *Columbia Law Review* 77 (November 1977), p. 1048, see the development of executive agreements as a major constitutional alteration which has been achieved by the executive branch, as opposed to the legislative or judicial branches.

8. Jethro K. Lieberman, *The Evolving Constitution* (New York: Random House, 1992), p. 192.

9. Barbara H. Craig and David M. O'Brien, *Abortion and American Politics* (Chatham, NJ: Chatham House Publishers, 1993), p. xiii.

10. Arguably, this dialogue is not as intense as it used to be. See James Q. Wilson's discussion of the differences between the "Old" and "New" political systems in the United States. *American Government: Brief Version*, 2d ed. (Lexington, MA: D.C. Heath, 1990), pp. 298–302. For evidence of some continuing vitality in this discussion, however, see Alpheus T. Mason, *The States Rights Debate: Antifederalism and the Constitution*, 2d ed. (New York: Oxford University Press, 1972).

11. For the Framers' intentions, see John R. Vile, *A Companion to the United States Constitution and Its Amendments* (Westport, CT: Praeger, 1993), p. 26.

12. James W. Ceaser, *Liberal Democracy and Political Science* (Baltimore, MD: Johns Hopkins University Press, 1990), p. 207.

13. "Clinton Compromises on Lifting Military Ban on Gays," *Facts on File* 53 (January 28, 1993), pp. 46–47.

14. Mike Mills, "Cost of Senate NIH Approval Is Continued Immigrant Ban," *Congressional Quarterly Weekly* 51 (February 20, 1993), p. 391.

15. See Lupu, "Statutes Revolving in Constitutional Law Orbits," pp. 37–52.

16. Cited by Alissa J. Rubin, "Freedom of Choice Bill Returns: Too Early To Predict Outcome," *Congressional Quarterly Weekly* 51 (March 20, 1993), p. 675.

17. Ibid., p. 52.

18. Adam Clymer, "Abortion-Rights Bill Gives Way to Other Priorities in Congress," *The New York Times* (September 16, 1993), pp. A1, A11.

19. See especially *Engel v. Vitale*, 370 U.S. 421 (1962), dealing with prayer in public schools and *Abingdon v. Schempp*, 374 U.S. 203 (1963) dealing with prayer and Bible reading.

20. *Widmar v. Vincent*, 454 U.S. 263 (1981).

21. *Board of Education of the Westside Community Schools v. Mergens*, 496 U.S. 226 (1990).

22. See Lupu, "Statutes Revolving in Constitutional Law Orbits," pp. 27–37. Lupu, p. 27, cites this legislation as embodying "the 'model of cooperation,' in which Congress built upon, and resolved conflicts among, existing judicial decisions."

23. Beth Donovan, "Clinton Reverses Directives; Battle Begins Anew," *Congressional Quarterly Weekly* 51 (January 23, 1993), p. 182.

24. *Rust v. Sullivan*, 111 S. Ct. 1759 (1991). The Reagan rules were themselves implemented by an administrative reinterpretation of laws administered by the Department of Health and Human Services. See Craig and O'Brien, *Abortion and American Politics*, pp. 188–91.

25. Craig and O'Brien, p. 355. This ban was originally established in the Reagan administration and maintained throughout the Bush presidency.

26. Anthony Lewis, *Make No Law: The Sullivan Case and the First Amendment* (New York: Random House, 1991), p. 58. Jefferson further commuted the sentences of those convicted under the Sedition Act, and Congress later reimbursed those who had been detained under this law. See Louis Fisher, "One of the Guardians Some of the Time," in *Is the Supreme Court the Guardian of the Constitution?*, ed. Robert A. Licht (Washington, DC: AEI Press, 1993), pp. 84–85.

27. *The Oxford Companion to the Supreme Court of the United States*, ed. Kermit L. Hall (New York: Oxford University Press, 1992), pp. 474–75.

28. *Harris v. McRae*, 448 U.S. 297 (1980). *Maher v. Roe*, 432 U.S. 464 (1977), had previously upheld a state's right to deny state funding for nontherapeutic abortions. For discussion of the Hyde Amendment, see Laurence H. Tribe, *The Clash of Absolutes* (New York: W. W. Norton, 1990), pp. 151–59.

29. Alissa J. Rubin with Jill Zuckman, "Abortion Funding Rebuff Shows House Divided," *Congressional Quarterly Weekly* 51 (July 3, 1993), pp. 1735–39.

30. For the argument that the American system is superior to parliamentary systems in this respect, see Ceaser, *Liberal Democracy and Political Science*, p. 204.

31. W. Craig Bledsoe and Margaret C. Thompson, "Executive Department," *Congressional Quarterly's Guide to the Presidency*, ed. Michael Nelson (Washington, DC: Congressional Quarterly, 1989), pp. 1001–002.

32. Robert E. DiClerico, *The American President*, 3d ed. (Englewood Cliffs, NJ: Prentice-Hall, 1990), p. 188.

33. See John Massaro, *Supremely Political: The Role of Ideology and Presidential Management in Unsuccessful Supreme Court Nominations* (Albany: State University of New York Press, 1990).

34. Another possibility is that Congress will attempt to reverse Supreme Court decisions through attempts to strip the Court of its jurisdiction. Two leading cases suggest different answers about the appropriateness of such procedures. See *Ex Parte McCardle*, 74 U.S. 506 (1869) and *United States v. Klein*, 80 U.S. 128 (1872). Since there have not been any recent exercises of the court-stripping power, this topic will not be discussed further in this book, but the possibility is ably treated in Louis Fisher and Neal Devins, *Political Dynamics of Constitutional Law* (St. Paul, MN: West Publishing, 1992), pp. 38–52.

35. Sue Davis has thus noted that "when the Court changes the Constitution, it does so only tentatively, pending final approval by Congress, the President, and

the states. Congress has the potential to interact with the judiciary in such a way as to provide substantial checks on the power of the Court. The interactive potential of the Court and Congress may be treated as a basis for the legitimacy of judicially amending the Constitution." See "Constitutional Change Through Judicial Review: A Dialectical View," paper prepared for presentation at the annual meeting of the Southwestern Social Science Association, San Antonio, Texas, March 1986, p. 6.

For another discussion of the various ways that Congress may respond to Court decisions, specifically focusing on labor and antitrust issues, see Beth M. Henschen and Edward I. Widlow, "The Supreme Court and the Congressional Agenda-Setting Process," *The Journal of Law & Politics* 5 (1989), pp. 685–724.

36. The author of one note counted twenty-one instances in the period from 1945 to 1957, which would be about two instances a year, but these figures may not necessarily be indicative of normal patterns. See "Congressional Reversal of Supreme Court Decisions: 1945–1956," *Harvard Law Review* 71 (1958), pp. 1324–37.

A more recent study suggests an average of about ten examples of statutory overrides per year, but the author of the study believes the 94th Congress represented a turning point, with approximately six overrides a year prior to this Congress and twelve per year thereafter. This study also suggests an increasing number of statutory overrides of lower court decisions. In reviewing cases of 1967 to 1990, the study found, however, that in only 4 percent of the decisions which Congress sought to overturn had the Court based its decisions on common and/or constitutional law reasoning. See William N. Eskridge, Jr., "Overriding Supreme Court Statutory Interpretation Decisions," *The Yale Law Journal* 101 (November 1991), pp. 338, 347.

37. 410 U.S. 113 (1973).

38. Tribe, *Abortion: The Clash of Absolutes*, p. 162. Legislation designed to "reverse" the Court's abortion decision or in the very least to get the Court to "reconsider" its decision is also ably discussed in Susan R. Burgess, *Contest for Constitutional Authority: The Abortion and War Powers Debates* (Lawrence: University Press of Kansas, 1992).

39. *Texas v. Johnson*, 491 U.S. 397 (1989).

40. Although a number of prominent law professors argued for this law, this writer, at least, suspects that they realized that such legislation would diffuse the clamor for a constitutional amendment and that, if, as it turned out, the new law was also declared unconstitutional, the amendment would then have less chance for success. See Mark E. Herrmann, "Looking Down from the Hill: Factors Determining the Success of Congressional Efforts to Reverse Supreme Court Interpretations of the Constitution," *William and Mary Law Review* 33 (Winter 1992), pp. 586–606.

41. *United States v. Eichman*, 496 U.S. 310 (1990).

42. *Civil Rights Cases*, 109 U.S. 3 (1883).

43. For a discussion of the congressional approach, see Herrmann, "Looking Down from the Hill," pp. 568–76.

44. 379 U.S. 241 (1964).

45. 379 U.S. 294 (1964). In his analysis of this and other laws specifically designed to overturn constitutional interpretations by the Supreme Court, Herrmann, "Looking Down from the Hill," pp. 606–7, has isolated a number of variables which appear to be especially important. These are "the extent to which Congress is able to disguise its motives; the gap in time, and resulting changes in the character of the Court, between the Court's action and the congressional response; Congress's ability to respond to concerns expressed in the Court's decision by basing its response on different constitutional grounds; the tone of congressional debate; the extent to which Congress has the cooperation of the states and/or the executive branch; and the nature of the constitutional issue involved."

46. See "Religious Freedom Bill OK'd," *The Christian Century* 110 (November 10, 1993), pp. 1116–17. Also see Lupu, "Statutes Revolving in Constitutional Law Orbits," pp. 52–66, and David Masci, "Religious Freedom Bill Wins Subcommittee Approval," *Congressional Quarterly Weekly* 51 (March 20, 1993), p. 676.

47. 494 U.S. 872 (1990). In deciding that the state was not required to apply the "compelling state interest test," the Court upheld a decision to disqualify members of the Native American Church from receiving unemployment insurance after they had been fired from their jobs as drug counselors for ingesting peyote as part of their religious practices.

Analyzing the law prior to its passage, Lupu argues, p. 62, that, despite its name, this law not only restores a previous conception of religious freedom, but that the freedom it restores "is of a variety far more potent than most of the pre-*Smith* case law would support." On p. 66, Lupu concludes that here, as in the case of the proposed Freedom of Choice Act, Congress would have "in judicial hands some very powerful tools with which to resist legislative efforts to redirect the flow of decision."

Decisions during the Court's 1992–93 session, most notably *Zobrest v. Catalina Foothills School District*, Docket 92–94 (1993)—involving use of a sign language interpreter in a parochial school—and *Church of the Lukumi Babalu Aye v. Hialeah* 113 S. Ct. 2217 (1993)—the Florida animal sacrifice case—might indicate that the Court was already in the process of reversing or modifying the *Smith* Decision prior to adoption of the Religious Freedom Restoration Act.

48. Thus, the author of "Congressional Reversal of Supreme Court Decisions," p. 1336, noted that of the twenty-one congressional reversals of Supreme Court opinions that he studied, "nearly all involved a return to a 'common understanding' which had been disrupted by the Court's decision, and that nearly all enjoyed the almost unanimous support of the politically articulate groups affected by the Court's decision." The author further observed that "those decisions that provoke a mixed reaction—and they must be far more numerous—are very rarely overruled by Congress."

49. 322 U.S. 533 (1944).

50. 75 U.S. 168 (1869).

51. *General Electric Co. v. Gilbert*, 429 U.S. 125 (1976).

52. Henry J. Abraham, *The Judiciary: The Supreme Court in the Governmental Process*, 8th ed. (Dubuque, IA: Wm C. Brown, 1991), p. 179.

53. *Garcia v. San Antonio Metropolitan Transit Authority*, 469 U.S. 528 (1985). This decision largely overturned the Court's earlier decision in *National League of Cities v. Usery*, 426 U.S. 833 (1976).

54. Ralph A. Rossum and G. Alan Tarr, *American Constitutional Law: Cases and Interpretation*, 3d ed. (New York: St. Martin's Press, 1991), p. 217.

55. *Goldman v. Weinberger*, 475 U.S. 503 (1986).

56. Fisher, "One of the Guardians Some of the Time," p. 96.

57. *Griggs v. Duke Power Co.*, 401 U.S. 424 (1971) and *Albemarle Paper Co. v. Moody*, 422 U.S. 405 (1975).

58. 490 U.S. 642 (1989).

59. See "The Civil Rights Act of 1991 and Less Discriminatory Alternatives in Disparate Impact Litigation," *Harvard Law Review* 106 (May 1993), pp. 1621–38.

60. The Supreme Court continued to recognize, however, that the president had authority to fire individuals not covered by this system. See *Myers v. United States*, 272 U.S. 52 (1926).

61. Stanley Kutler, "Impoundment Powers," *The Oxford Companion to the Supreme Court of the United States*, ed. Kermit L. Hall (New York: Oxford University Press, 1992), p. 425.

62. W. Craig Bledsoe and James B. Watts, "Chief Executive," *Congressional Quarterly's Guide to the Presidency*, ed. Michael Nelson (Washington, DC: Congressional Quarterly, 1989), p. 423.

63. The Resolution thus states that "Nothing in this joint resolution—(1) is intended to alter the constitutional authority of the Congress or of the President, or of the provisions of existing treaties." See Rossum and Tarr, *American Constitutional Law*, p. 172.

64. *Immigration and Naturalization Service v. Chadha*, 462 U.S. 919 (1983).

65. See the decision in *Crockett v. Reagan*, 558 F. Supp. 893 (1982) rejecting justiciability over the constitutionality of the administration's military actions in El Salvador.

66. See J. Woodford Howard, Jr., "War Powers Act of 1973," in *The Oxford Companion to the Supreme Court of the United States*, ed. Kermit L. Hall (New York: Oxford University Press, 1992), pp. 911–12. Quotation is from p. 912. For further discussion of this law, see Burgess, *Contest for Constitutional Authority*.

67. Daniel C. Diller and Dean J. Peterson, "Chief Economist," *Guide to the Presidency*, ed. Michael Nelson (Washington, DC: Congressional Quarterly, 1989), pp. 653–56.

68. For discussion of this amendment and related budget issues, see *The Constitution and the Budget*, ed. W. S. Moore and Rudolph G. Penner (Washington, DC: American Enterprise Institute for Public Policy Research, 1980).

69. This attempt was, of course, invalidated (at least insofar as it sought to interfere with qualifications in state elections), in *Oregon v. Mitchell*, 400 U.S. 112 (1970).

70. Michael Nelson, ed., *Congressional Quarterly's Guide to the Presidency* (Washington, DC: Congressional Quarterly, 1989), p. 482.

71. Ibid.

72. Reagan's victories, in particular, call into question the widespread idea that government in Washington is in perpetual gridlock and cannot govern. Along similar lines, see David R. Mayhew, *Divided We Govern* (New Haven, CT: Yale University Press, 1991).

73. 384 U.S. 641 (1966). Also see *Oregon v. Mitchell*, 400 U.S. 112 (1970).

74. *Lassiter v. Northhampton County Board of Elections*, 360 U.S. 45 (1959).

75. The Autumn 1993 issue of *Law and Contemporary Problems* consists of a symposium entitled "Elected Branch Influences in Constitutional Decisionmaking." Scholars who are interested in the role of the electoral branches influencing constitutional interpretation will find this symposium to be especially useful. Of special value are the articles by Geoffrey P. Miller entitled "The President's Power of Interpretation: Implications of a Unified Theory of Constitutional Law," pp. 35–62 and Roger H. Davidson, "The Lawmaking Congress," pp. 99–120. The symposium also contains a number of case studies.

Chapter 5

Examining the Terminology and Theory of Constitutional Change

If the thesis of this book is correct, there are at least three peaceful ways to effect changes in the U.S. constitutional order—an order which includes both the capital *C* and lowercase *c* constitutions. The formal amending process of Article V may initiate change, the judiciary may initiate change, or one or both of the elected branches may initiate change. Each method of change is real, and each has its own strengths and weaknesses. This author will examine these in the next chapter. In this chapter, the author will survey some of the existing terminology which describes change and assess the adequacy of existing theories that attempt to explain it.

THE TERMINOLOGY OF LEGAL CHANGE

Writers on constitutional change draw a number of distinctions, but these distinctions are difficult to compare because they are directed to different objectives.[1] Some classifications distinguish the formal Article V processes from other forms of change, whereas other nomenclatures measure the degree of change effected through whatever mechanism is utilized. Moreover, the two purposes tend to blend into one another, thus obscuring their different foci.

Donald S. Lutz focuses on distinguishing formal constitutional amendments from other forms of change, and, to this end, he utilizes the distinction between *amendment* and *revision*.[2] In his initial typology, he classifies changes inaugurated through the formal Article V process as amendments, and he designates changes initiated by the three branches of government, and especially the judicial branch, as constitutional revisions. Recognizing that the two processes are closely interrelated, Lutz hypothesizes that "A low amendment rate, associated with a long average constitutional duration, strongly implies the use of some alternate means of revision to supplement the formal amending process."[3] The most fascinating aspect of Lutz's analysis may be that while, as in the above quotation, he uses terminology fairly consistently, he subsequently uses the term *amendment* not simply to designate changes initiated through formal Article V processes but also to distinguish major and minor changes. Thus, at one point, he argues:

> *As long as interpretation does not move outside a range of possibilities defined by a normal language interpretation of constitutional provision*, even if the operation of the political system is significantly changed as a consequence, there has not really been an amendment but rather a specification of a choice within a range of possibilities.[4]

Lutz's reservation suggests that he might find it difficult to maintain a merely formal distinction between amendment and interpretation in cases where one of the three branches of government exceeds the ordinary bounds of interpretation.

By contrast to the general direction of Lutz's classification scheme, Sanford Levinson expresses less interest in separating Article V processes from others than in distinguishing differing degrees of change. Levinson distinguishes between *interpretation* and *amendment*.[5] On the surface, this classification seems similar to Levinson's distinction between *revision* and *amendment*. Rather than differentiating between change instituted through constitutional amendment or through other means, however, Levinson uses *interpretation* to symbolize "ordinary development" and *amendment* to stand for "extraordinary development,"[6] the first referring to changes already implicit within the constitutional scheme and the second to changes that are not so implicit: "The contrast between interpretation and amendment is akin to that between organic development and the *invention* of entirely new solutions to old problems."[7] By Levinson's analysis, then, certain changes which Article V processes initiate come closer to interpretations than to amendments (since their principles have already been implicit within the text), whereas some judicial interpretations like *McCulloch v. Maryland*[8] should actually be understood as "*de facto* amendment[s]."[9] Not surprisingly, while Lutz's scheme of classification is relatively straightforward, Levinson ends up with five different categories of change[10] and ultimately acknowledges that he "cannot provide formal criteria" by which to distinguish interpretations from amendments.[11] Indeed, following the analysis of Walter Murphy and other scholars,[12] Levinson hypothesizes that some constitutional changes which might be effected through Article V would be so radical that they could not properly qualify as amendments.[13]

Stephen Markman, a conservative advocate of the doctrine of original intent and an opponent of judicial activism, comes closer to Levinson's classification scheme than to Lutz's, but his central thrust is critical and normative rather than descriptive. Like Levinson, Markman apparently believes that changes effected by amendment are changes of a certain order. For Markman, the fact that the Constitution specifies only one formal amending process indicates that this process should be the exclusive mechanism for certain types of change—namely, those interpretations either inconsistent with, or not mandated by, the original intent of the Constitution's Framers.[14] Markman thus notes that Article V is "the sole mode of amendment permitted by the Constitution."[15] He further states:

> Article V of the Constitution is the definitive articulation of the idea that the Constitution is not "written on water"; that its meaning is not to evolve and "mature" over time[;] that judges are not to do "justice," but are to do "justice under law"; that it matters what the Founders intended their work to mean. Article V of the Constitution is the ultimate expression that the Constitution is not a "mere parchment barrier," but that its guarantees and principles are permanent and unchanging in the absence of formal constitutional amendments. It mandates that constitutional intent, unless altered through Article V's exacting process, shall remain the original intent.[16]

Again, Markman's terminology is not as precise as Levinson's, but Markman believes that certain important changes in constitutional understandings, somewhat imprecisely dubbed "amendments," should only be effected through Article V processes.[17]

Although their article was written earlier in time, Stephen Munzer and James Nickel have offered something of a compromise among the above views. Like the author of this book, they acknowledge that amendments, judicial interpretations, and legislative and executive actions all contribute to constitutional change. In addition, they distinguish among three types of judicial change—those in which the courts fill in "an *openness* in constitutional provisions," those (and here Levinson's category of "revision" seems similar) where the courts proceed on the assumption that the Constitution is "a living organism that grows," and those occasions where the judicial innovation is so great that it should be considered a type of *"reauthoring* or informal amendment."[18] Through use of the term *informal amendment*, Munzer and Nickel thus continue to distinguish between amendments enacted through Article V processes and changes initiated in other ways.[19] Unlike Markman, who distinguishes between judicial interpretation and judicial innovation, Munzer and Nickel think there are occasions where informal amendment through judicial decisions may be appropriate.[20]

Peter Suber utilizes an approach similar to that of Munzer and Nickel. Acknowledging that the power of judicial interpretation effectively allows the judiciary to engage in lawmaking, he notes that the judiciary can also "amend law."[21] Suber prefers to designate changes which stretch or contravene the boundaries of legislative intent "judicial amendments," a heading he uses to avoid "the broad connotation of unqualified 'amendments' and the timidity of 'quasi-' or 'virtual' amendments."[22]

BROADER THEORIES OF CONSTITUTIONAL CHANGE

While the theorists discussed above primarily distinguished among different forms of constitutional change, other theorists have formulated broader theories of change. None has received more attention than Bruce Ackerman whose initial book is part of a projected series of three volumes that Sanford Levinson has praised as "the most significant work in constitutional theory to be published in this decade, . . . indeed, perhaps in the past half-century."[23]

While it is difficult to do justice even to Ackerman's initial volume in short compass, his most original contribution to the amending debate is probably his thesis that America is a "dualist democracy" where periods of ordinary lawmaking are periodically interrupted by periods of "higher lawmaking" or *"constitutional politics"*[24] which constitute distinct "constitutional moment[s]." Altogether, Ackerman identifies three successful transitions to new regimes initiated through these constitutional moments, as well as a number of lesser moments where substantial changes were also initiated. The writing of the U.S. Constitution, the Civil War, and the New Deal initiated these three primary regimes.[25] Moreover, Ackerman thinks it is especially significant that the normal Article V amending procedure did not initiate any of these regimes. The authors of the Constitution specified a new procedure rather than following the one specified in the Articles of Confederation. The proponents of the post–Civil War amendments effectively forced the Southern states to ratify them as a condition for renewed congressional representation.[26] Finally, the changes the New Deal initiated were never formally incorporated into the Constitution.

In examining each of these three "constitutional moments," and especially the New Deal, Ackerman concludes that, contrary to much existing constitutional mythology, these were real and important changes and not simple returns to earlier constitutional interpretations. Moreover, major changes followed a discrete series of stages. First was the "signaling phase" during which the movement moved to the center stage of public attention. Next was the "proposal" stage where a series of reforms were formulated. This was followed by a period of "mobilized popular deliberation," and, if successful, by "legal [albeit not necessarily uppercase *C* constitutional] codification."[27] By such a formulation—which is, however, designed to focus more on regime transformations than on more ordinary periods of what Ackerman calls "normal politics"[28]—Ackerman has widened those traditional narratives of change which have focused primarily on the judicial branch.[29] By the same token, Ackerman has arguably moved the formal Article V amending process to the periphery of the discussion, its place now taken by changes in public opinion, by controversies surrounding confirmation hearings,[30] by elections, and by accommodations by the political branches.

James Pope has supplemented Ackerman's analysis by focusing on "republican moments."[31] Pope thereby somewhat democratizes the notion of popularly inspired changes by expanding their number, but his argument otherwise corresponds fairly closely to Ackerman's idea of "constitutional moments."[32] Thus, in plotting what he calls "the development of civil society," Pope shows horizontal periods of "politics-as-usual" alternating with vertical "republican moments" in a kind of stair-step arrangement which is presumably headed in a progressive direction.[33]

While Pope's analysis, like Ackerman's, relegates the role of the amending process to the periphery, a particularly fascinating aspect of Pope's thinking is that he suggests an interpretative principle which ties constitutional changes to a principle of judicial interpretation. Thus, he argues that "statutes that result from higher track lawmaking—call them republican statutes—should receive a broad construction; products of interest group bargaining should . . . be narrowly constructed."[34] On the negative side, Pope overlooks the problem of interpreting a narrowly drawn statute (or amendment) which resulted from higher lawmaking more expansively than a broadly worded statute which is not such a product. Moreover, Pope probably underestimates the degree to which such an interpretative principle, if consistently applied, would make it more difficult to enact "higher lawmaking statutes" for fear of inviting increased judicial intervention.[35]

Both Ackerman and Pope perceive that the processes of change are sporadic and that when changes come they often come in clusters, with some changes being significantly more important than others. Thus, periods of normal politics typically follow so-called republican or constitutional moments. With a similar sense that change is an intermittent process, Robert Lipkin has enunciated a somewhat different view. It centers on a model of constitutional revolutions[36] largely patterned after Thomas Kuhn's now classic formulation of scientific revolutions.[37] Like such revolutions, Lipkin argues that constitutional periods are shaped by the formulation of new paradigms which determine how problems are most appropriately conceptualized.[38] The development of such a paradigm is followed by a period of "normal adjudication," in which "members of the legal community . . . define relevant facts, constitutional questions, appropriate analytic frameworks, arguments, conclusions and remedies,"[39] and, eventually, by a new paradigm.

Perhaps because he has so emphasized the difficulty and so disparaged the efficacy of the formal amending process,[40] Lipkin insists that the engine of constitutional revolution is "a judicial decision establishing a model for disposing of constitutional cases in that area of law."[41] Similarly, he describes "judges," rather than the people or their elected representatives, as the primary actors in the process.[42] Moreover, Lipkin lists numerous revolutionary decisions throughout American history, insisting that such cases as *Marbury v. Madison* (1803), *Martin v. Hunter's Lessee* (1816), and a host of others—while possibly consistent with "the best and most likely conception of federalism"[43]—did "not flow from the text, intent, history, structure or logic of the Constitution."[44] Lipkin believes that John Marshall and other constitutional interpreters have read their own political philosophies into the Constitution "under the guise of constitutionalism" and that the process of constitutional interpretation is "overwhelmingly political."[45]

While Lipkin thinks constitutional change is important, he focuses almost entirely on the role of the judicial branch in both initiating and subsequently codifying legal change. Not only does he thereby denigrate the role of the formal processes of Article V, but he also writes as though the dynamic of change is a completely elitist project which proceeds independent of popular input. However well he might thus explain one form of constitutional change, perhaps even at times the dominant form, his overall effort is arguably no more satisfactory than accounts which focus exclusively on Article V amendments alone or on popularly inspired constitutional moments.

ANALYSIS

The primary difficulty with existing theories of constitutional change arguably stems from the twin facts that changes come in so many gradations and may be instituted and/or frustrated by any number of actors. In the United States, change may be registered in laws or orders, judicial decisions, and/or in constitutional amendments, and a reading of the written Constitution thus does not always lead to insights into the actual working constitution of government and the changes it has undergone. Moreover, a theory that explains major changes may not recognize or explain more mundane ones, while a theory that focuses on changes initiated through one mechanism may not effectively explain those effected through the others.

Ackerman has successfully widened the theory of constitutional change to include more than the formal Article V amending procedures,[46] and he has been especially successful in integrating social and legal changes together. In attempting to explain major constitutional transformations, however, it is doubtful that he has also explained more mundane processes of change, and, even in explaining major transformations, he has arguably underestimated both the role that the Article V amending process has often had in initiating and/or in legitimizing such transformations. Thus, while ignoring the requirement of the Articles of Confederation for unanimous consent by the state legislatures, the framers of the U.S. Constitution effectively threw themselves on the mercy of their constituents and attempted to inaugurate a more regularized and effective process for inaugurating future changes. Moreover, the irregularities surrounding the post–Civil War amendments may ultimately be less important than the fact that American leaders decided to incorporate such alterations into the written (uppercase) Constitution. Similarly, some aspects of the New Deal revolution may ultimately prove to be insecure because their proponents never used the Article V processes to incorporate them into the text of the Constitution.[47]

In attempting to widen the application of Ackerman's theory, Pope has arguably moved the amending process even farther to the periphery. Lipkin makes a similar mistake, albeit shifting his emphasis from actions of the elected branches to actions of the judiciary. Undoubtedly, both Ackerman's and Lipkin's theories apply fairly well to certain periods of U.S. history. Both writers seem, however, to have described one method for change and portrayed it as exclusive.

Lutz, Levinson, Munzer and Nickel, and Suber may have come closest to recognizing that constitutional changes do not necessarily follow a pre-set pattern but may be instituted in a variety of ways, each of which influences the others. Their theories also suggest that it may be more appropriate to institute some changes through one mechanism rather than through others, but, no one as yet appears to have fashioned a comprehensive theory of which kinds of changes are best instituted through each mechanism.

AN ALTERNATIVE APPROACH

Rather than aim for such a grand theory, this author has decided to try an alternate and more empirical tack. He begins with the premise, somewhat contrary to that of Stephen Markman and Robert Lipkin, that, historical practice having been what it has been, there are three relatively well-established means of initiating constitutional change in the United States and that, at least in some circumstances, each is legitimate. He further posits that each of these mechanisms has certain strengths and weaknesses and that a comparison of these strengths and weaknesses is most likely to lead, at least tentatively, to a consideration of when each mechanism for change is most appropriate. This is the task of the next chapter.

NOTES

1. This author has discussed a number of the theorists addressed in this chapter in chapter 5 of *Contemporary Questions Surrounding the Constitutional Amending Process* (Westport, CT: Praeger, 1993), but readers should be able to detect an evolution in his own thought as well as perceiving the different emphases of each chapter.

2. Donald S. Lutz, "Toward a Theory of Constitutional Amendment," paper presented at the American Political Science Convention, Chicago, Illinois, September 1992, p. 6. In a similar fashion, when discussing the Supreme Court's powers of judicial review, Louis Lusky subtitled his book *A Commentary of the Supreme Court's Power to* Revise *the Constitution* (emphasis mine). See *By What Right* (Charlottesville, VA: Mickie Company, 1975).

3. Ibid., p. 40.

4. Ibid., p. 8. Emphasis mine.

5. Sanford Levinson, "Accounting for Constitutional Change (Or, How Many Times Has the United States Constitution Been Amended? (A) < 26; (B) 26; (C) > 26; (D) All of the Above," *Constitutional Commentary* 8 (Summer 1991), p. 411.

6. Ibid.

7. Ibid., p. 411. For a similar formulation, see Sanford Levinson, "On the Notion of Amendment: Reflections on David Daube's Jehovah the Good," *S'Vara: A Journal of Philosophy and Judaism* 1 (Winter 1990), pp. 25–31.

8. 4 Wheat (17 U.S.) 316 (1819).

9. Levinson, "Accounting for Constitutional Change," p. 419.

10. Ibid., p. 417. They range from an " 'interpretation' of what was already immanent within the existing body of legal materials" to "a change of such fundamental dimension as to be called truly revolutionary and thus taken out of the language of amendment at all."

11. Ibid., p. 428.

12. Such views are cited and analyzed in Vile, *Contemporary Questions*, chapter 7.

13. Levinson, "Accounting for Constitutional Change," p. 417.

14. Markman's view appears to be quite similar to views espoused by political conservatives earlier in this century. See Thomas H. Peebles, "A Call to High Debate: The Organic Constitution in Its Formative Era, 1890–1920," *University of Colorado Law Review* 52 (Fall 1980), pp. 83–88.

15. Stephen J. Markman, "The Jurisprudence of Constitutional Amendments," in *Still the Law of the Land?*, ed. Joseph S. McNamara and Lissa Roche (Hillsdale, MI: Hillsdale College Press, 1987), p. 87. Markman would be on stronger ground if he were to argue that Article V is the sole mode of amendment specifically outlined by the Constitution.

16. Ibid., p. 95. Also see Stephen J. Markman, "The Amendment Process of Article V: A Microcosm of the Constitution," *Harvard Journal of Law & Public Policy* 12 (1989), pp. 113–21.

17. The fact that Markman is critiquing existing judicial practice, however, suggests that he is aware that, by his definition, the courts *do* currently *amend* the Constitution but that he thinks either that they *should* not have the authority or that they should not exercise such authority.

Markman presents a well-argued brief for the advantages of utilizing the formal Article V processes over judicial interpretations by focusing in "The Jurisprudence of Constitutional Amendments," pp. 91–92, and in "The Amendment Process," pp. 117–18, chiefly on considerations of federalism, separation of powers, and democracy. Stripped of its partisanship and expanded to include other relevant comparative measures, this author has found this approach to be suggestive in formulating his own comparisons of alternative methods of constitutional change in the chapter which follows.

18. Stephen R. Munzer and James. W. Nickel, "Does the Constitution Mean What It Always Meant?" *Columbia Law Review* 77 (November 1977), pp. 1045–46.

19. Stephen Keogh uses similar terminology but professes to be following the theories of Bruce Ackerman in so doing. See Keogh's, "Formal and Informal Constitutional Lawmaking in the United States in the Winter of 1860–1861," *Journal of Legal History* 8 (December 1987), pp. 275–99.

20. Ibid., p. 1061. Munzer and Nickel noted: "If constitutional change is believed necessary on the basis of careful consideration and careful argumentation, and if an authoritative interpreter has good grounds for believing that the change will not be introduced through formal amendment, innovation of this radical sort may then be desirable."

Somewhat along the same line, Alex Kozinski and Eugene Volokh have argued both that, "Like it or not, our constitutional law is the law of penumbras and emanations," and that "penumbras and emanations are dangerous business." See "A Penumbra Too Far," *Harvard Law Review* 106 (May 1993), pp. 1656–57.

21. Peter Suber, *The Paradox of Self-Amendment* (New York: Peter Lang, 1990), p. 197.

22. Ibid., p. 198.

23. Bruce Ackerman, *We the People: Foundations* (Cambridge, MA: Harvard University Press, Belknap Press, 1991). The projected volumes are to be respectively titled *Transformations* and *Interpretations*. Levinson's quotation is found on the paper flyleaf of the clothbound edition of Ackerman's book.

24. Ibid., p. 7.

25. Ibid., p. 40.

26. For a writer who has emphasized the ties between the changes inaugurated after the Civil War and the philosophy of the American Revolution, see David A. J. Richards, "Revolution and Constitutionalism in America," *Cardozo Law Review* 14 (January 1993), pp. 577–634.

27. Ibid., pp. 266–67.

28. Ibid., p. 230, chapter title.

29. Ackerman says one of his goals is "to move beyond the court-centered view that afflicts the modern professional narrative" and says that his primary unit of analysis is "the constitutional regime, the matrix of institutional relationships and fundamental values that are usually taken as the constitutional baseline in normal political life." Ibid., p. 59.

30. See Bruce Ackerman's, "Transformative Appointments," *Harvard Law Review* 101 (1988), pp. 1164–84.

31. James G. Pope, "Republican Moments: The Role of Direct Popular Power in the American Constitutional Order," *University of Pennsylvania Law Review* 139 (December 1990), pp. 287–368.

32. For Pope's description of the five features that characterize republican moments, see p. 311.

33. Ibid., p. 319.

34. Ibid., p. 360. On p. 361, Pope associates republican statutes with: "(1) widespread and serious public discussion; (2) debate framed in terms of principle and public good; (3) an intention to bring about major changes in the legal

order; (4) direct citizen action, such as social protest; and (5) extensive activity by voluntary associations and social movements."

35. William Van Alstyne thus attributes the defeat of the proposed Equal Rights Amendment to "fear of congressional capture, and the conjecture that the Supreme Court would too readily acquiesce in such uses as Congress might presume to make of its new authority." See Van Alstyne, "Notes on a Bicentennial Constitution: Part I, Processes of Change," *University of Illinois Law Review* (1984), p. 957.

36. Robert J. Lipkin, "The Anatomy of Constitutional Revolutions," *Nebraska Law Review* 68 (1989), p. 728, defines a "constitutional revolution" as "a legal change not clearly authorized by the Constitution." This definition seems to be similar to Levinson's definition of an *amendment* ("the *invention* of entirely new solutions to old problems"), *supra*, note 6, although, with its reference to "not *clearly* authorized," Lipkin's definition arguably forces a "revolutionary" heading on changes not stated in, but consistent with, a Constitution.

Lipkin argues that the process of constitutional revolution "is an alternative process of amending the Constitution," necessitated by the difficulty of the formal amending process. See pp. 728–29.

37. *The Structure of Scientific Revolutions*, 2d ed. (Chicago: University of Chicago Press, 1970).

38. Lipkin, p. 734, says that a constitutional paradigm determines: "(1) the type of facts that give rise to the relevant constitutional question; (2) the standard of review to be employed; (3) the analytic framework for discussing and evaluating the facts; (4) the rules of law to be applied; and (5) the available remedies."

39. Ibid., p. 739.

40. Ibid., pp. 728–29. Lipkin notes that "the process of constitutional revolution is an alternative process of amending the Constitution." He further notes that "this Article presupposes that any constitutional scheme, or system of practical rules, not having an easily assessable formal process of amendment, will develop an alternative revolutionary process. The formal amendment process in American constitutionalism is difficult to deploy, hence, revolutionary adjudication is inevitable."

41. Ibid., p. 740.

42. Ibid., p. 746.

43. Ibid., p. 761.

44. Ibid., p. 757. Lipkin uses this terminology specifically when referring to *Martin v. Hunter's Lessee*, 14 U.S. 304 (1816).

As noted in footnote 35 above, Lipkin's definition labels as "revolutionary" changes that in other schemes might be regarded as immanent, if not explicitly stated, within the constitutional text.

45. Ibid., pp. 773, 775.

46. Clement Vose's highly useful book, *Constitutional Change: Amendment Politics and Supreme Court Litigation Since 1900* (Lexington, MA: Lexington Books, 1972) has fulfilled a similar function in analyzing constitutional amend-

ments and Supreme Court decisions within the same historical narrative, but he offers no real theory of how such procedures are related and arguably underestimates the effect of the two political branches in initiating change.

47. David E. Kyvig, "The Road Not Taken: FDR, the Supreme Court, and Constitutional Amendment," *Political Science Quarterly* 104 (Fall 1989), p. 481.

Chapter 6

Laws, Orders, Judicial Decisions, and Amendments: A Comparative Analysis

Previous chapters have identified and described three major sources of change in the interpretation of America's formal Constitution and in the larger constitutional scheme of which it is a part. These chapters have also pointed to the ways that these mechanisms overlap and interact with one another.

This chapter will assess the strengths and weaknesses of each of these three mechanisms. In comparing the respective advantages and disadvantages of these processes, this author will utilize a number of sometimes overlapping dimensions which appear to be the most relevant and most prominent in the literature.[1]

EASE

Of all the routes toward constitutional change, the amending route is undoubtedly the most difficult. It requires not only two-thirds majorities in both houses of Congress (the vote that would also be needed to override a presidential veto of an ordinary piece of legislation), but also the concurrence of three-fourths of the states.[2] Undoubtedly, this difficulty helps account both for the paucity of amendments that have been ratified and for the reluctance that advocates of change have to pursue this method when other alternatives are available.[3] The difficulty of the process can, however, be deceptive in its implications for individual amendments, sometimes leading people to exaggerate the difficulties. Thus, in the early

1920s a senator declared that "there is as much chance of repealing the Eighteenth Amendment as there is for a hummingbird to fly to the planet Mars with the Washington Monument tied to its tail,"[4] and yet the states ratified just such an amendment in 1933.

The number of federal laws and executive orders, as well as a number of examples cited earlier in this book, demonstrate that the processes of law-making and issuing executive orders are considerably easier than the amending process. Thus, Congress successfully adopted a law banning desecration of the flag, but it never mustered sufficient majorities to propose an amendment on the subject. Similarly, while Congress passed a law providing for equal access of religious groups in high schools, it has never reported out a prayer-in-school amendment.

The ease of legislation, however, is only comparative. While scholars have undoubtedly sometimes exaggerated the extent of legislative "gridlock,"[5] such claims testify to the many obstacles to the adoption of legislation in a system that provides for bicameralism, separation of powers, and checks and balances, factors that are arguably exaggerated by current institutional arrangements (e.g., the dispersion of power among committee chairs and weak party loyalty) within Congress itself. Moreover, once Congress overcomes such obstacles, legislation still has to pass the barrier of judicial review. In some cases, the above-mentioned law dealing with flag desecration, for example, this barrier is fatal.

In contrast to both amendments and legislation, judicially initiated changes may appear easy indeed. A change in the interpretation of law by the Supreme Court can require a switch in anywhere from one to five votes, depending on the majority which upholds an existing interpretation. The most likely, albeit not the sole, cause of such a change in votes is a change in judicial personnel. Although some presidents have served an entire term without making a single appointment, Presidents Jimmy Carter and Franklin Roosevelt, for example, most presidents get at least one such chance. Apart from the possibility that a member of the Supreme Court might change his or her mind, a president seeking to reverse a five-to-four decision who chooses his appointees wisely may thus be able to effect change relatively quickly. Absent a change of heart by sitting members of the Court, a president seeking to reverse a nine-to-zero or an eight-to-one decision would typically require at least two terms in office as well as judicial appointees willing to carry out the president's own views.[6]

Faced with an initial opinion legalizing abortion by a six-to-two vote (with both dissenters continuing on the Court), Presidents Reagan and Bush appointed five justices between them and elevated one sitting member to Chief Justice and yet still found a reversal of *Roe v. Wade* eluding them by a five-to-four margin.[7] A president might try, as Franklin Roosevelt once did, to "pack" the Supreme Court by having Congress authorize new justices,[8] but, given Roosevelt's disappointing experience with this mechanism, the likelihood of this happening today is probably as remote as it ever was. As Roosevelt's eventual triumph also shows, however, judicial reversal is generally more likely than is adoption of a constitutional amendment.

The comparative ease of judicial reversal has a number of drawbacks. If exercised too frequently, particularly in the absence of major changes that would justify a judicial about-face, this ease may undermine respect for the law, by furthering the perception that most decisions are politically motivated.[9] Similarly, the use of judicial interpretation to bring about desirable change in one area of the law may make resort to this mechanism more likely in less desirable cases. This was Thomas Jefferson's fear regarding the Louisiana Purchase and expansive readings of the Constitution more generally. If the Constitution were given a broad construction for a desirable policy, it might later be so constructed for an undesirable one.[10]

RANGE

Only one stated limit on the constitutional amending process is applicable today,[11] and, if there are any unstated limits, they are surely not extensive.[12] Potentially, then, there is little, if anything, that a substantial segment of the population desires that it cannot effect through amendment if it can mobilize the necessary congressional and state majorities to that end. The people have thus adopted amendments to protect and expand individual rights, to extend voting rights, to institute and repeal national alcoholic prohibition, and to make minor repairs in existing constitutional structures.[13] The range of proposed amendments, however, has been considerably more extensive.[14] Any real limits on the constitutional amending process are likely to be ones (such as that illustrated by the failure of the Eighteenth Amendment) which inhere in the inability of certain types of laws to command widespread obedience rather than limits which are constitutionally imposed or implied.

Few areas of modern everyday life are unaffected by congressional legislation and/or executive orders. Such laws and orders undoubtedly cover a wider range of subjects than do constitutional amendments. From a constitutional standpoint, however, the Constitution and judicial interpretations of that document constrain all such laws and orders. Under current judicial interpretations, there are areas of the law (e.g., authority to legislate over economic matters) where such constraints are relatively insubstantial; in other areas (e.g., those mentioned in the *Carolene Products* footnote)[15] such restraints are fairly formidable. Constitutional restraints and judicial limitations on legislative and executive action within a given area can be so clear and precise as virtually to preclude effective response through these mechanisms. As minor a change as moving the times that new members of Congress and new presidents took office required a constitutional amendment because this change altered the constitutionally established terms of the officeholders in power at the time.[16]

Scholars certainly disagree about the extent to which judicial interpretations can or should be constrained by such factors as the plain meaning of words, the original intent of the Framers, precedent, and the like,[17] but even the most liberal commentator does not argue that judges should roam at will with no attention to the existing constitutional landscape. If the rule of law is to be meaningful, justices must, in the very least, render decisions consistent with the interpretive community of which they are a part. While a number of broad phrases in the Constitution give fairly free range to judicial decision making, the specificity of some constitutional language—like that providing for the four-year presidential term and the specification of the number of senators from each state, for example,[18]—effectively precludes extensive alteration. Widely accepted judicial maxims such as the case and controversy requirement, the requirements for standing, the political questions doctrine, limitations on taxpayer suits, and so on[19] also sometimes preclude issues from reaching the courts or being decided by them.[20]

As will be discussed in a later section of this chapter devoted to efficacy, literature has also increasingly demonstrated that, as with orders issued by the president,[21] there is sometimes a gap between what justices decree and what actually happens.[22] It is a long-standing truism that the Court exercises the power of neither the purse nor the sword,[23] but the observation is no less important on that account.

DIRECTION

This book has stressed that amendments, judicial decisions, and laws and executive orders may direct change toward the unknown, or they may attempt to preserve the existing status quo or return to a prior state of affairs. Since only one amendment has repealed another, it would seem clear that amendments generally point in the direction of the unknown, but there are two reservations that need to be made about such an observation. First, to the extent that some amendments—the Eleventh and Twelfth, for example—were adopted to correct an unanticipated defect in constitutional procedure or an unanticipated interpretation of that document, they too point back to a known or anticipated standard. Second, a number of amendments—the Seventeenth, Eighteenth, and Twenty-Sixth, for example—have been "pretested" at the state level.

Like amendments, laws and executive orders can direct change toward an unknown but anticipated future or back toward a previous state of affairs. Generally, the elected branches are most likely to initiate changes in new directions, albeit subject to the constraints imposed by existing constitutional structures and interpretations.[24]

Judicial decisions are as versatile as any other kinds of changes, but, if the analysis earlier in this book is correct, radical judicial change in a new direction is controversial precisely because it is so extraordinary. The felt need of most members of the Court to justify departures from *stare decisis*, as well as the criticisms that are directed to the Court for judicial activism, both indicate that the most typical and uncontroversial judicial role is preservation of the status quo. Robert Lipkin's analysis as described in the previous chapter would further indicate that periods of judicial innovation where new principles are developed or implemented are typically followed by periods of more routine or normal adjudication.[25]

SPEED

It is not easy to compare the speed with which constitutional amendments and other forms of constitutional change can be effected because this speed is likely to vary significantly from one issue to another. The only physical limitation on the speed with which amendments may be adopted is the time needed to pass a resolution by two-thirds majorities in both houses of Congress which can subsequently be ratified by three-fourths of the state legislatures or special conventions called for this purpose.[26] Similarly, the only physical limitation on the speed by which changes can be initiated by Congress is imposed by the time it takes to get a bill adopted by both houses of Congress and either signed by the president or re-adopted over his veto.[27] The only physical limitation on the speed with which the judicial branch can act definitively is the time it takes to initiate a case (or for the Court to accept such a case already on the lower court dockets) and appeal it to the Supreme Court.

From the time Congress has proposed the first twenty-six amendments, the states have ratified them in time periods ranging from less than three and a half months (the Twenty-Sixth Amendment)[28] to as long as three years and eleven months (the Twenty-Second Amendment).[29] In a special category of one is the putative Twenty-Seventh Amendment, which Congress first proposed in 1789 as part of the package which became the Bill of Rights, and which the states did not ratify until 1992.[30] The people have often, however, debated amendments for years before they were proposed, the Seventeenth Amendment[31] and the Nineteenth Amendment[32] being good cases in point. In recent years, Congress has usually specified a seven-year ratification deadline for amendments. In an action that is still controversial, Congress extended this period an additional three years and three months in the case of the proposed Equal Rights Amendment.[33]

Laws and executive orders, like judicial modifications of constitutional law—the 1937 "switch in time," for example—sometimes appear much more abrupt, but such laws, orders, and decisions often culminate decades of judicial developments, as studies of cases like *Brown v. Board of Education*[34] and *Gideon v. Wainwright*[35] demonstrate. In short, the time involved in the amending process, the legislative and executive processes, and the judicial processes can be highly variable; on occasion, all can act quickly; at other times, they may result from decades of discussion.

VISIBILITY

One advantage of the formal constitutional amending process is that, like the act by which the U.S. Constitution was originally ratified, it is one of the most visible acts in the polity,[36] an act by which the public clearly knows that a change in constitutional law has been effected. In this respect, the process of amendment reflects more generally the advantages inherent in a written Constitution. What does the Constitution say? It is arguably easier, especially for the lay person, to look at the text of the Constitution to find an answer than at a multiplicity of judicial pronouncements.[37]

Provisions incorporated into the nation's written Constitution arguably also have a greater chance of influencing public opinion than those which are not. Thus, in responding to Thomas Jefferson's plea to incorporate a bill of rights into the Constitution, James Madison, whose attitude was otherwise fairly tepid toward this prospect, agreed that "the political truths declared in that solemn manner acquire by degrees the character of fundamental maxims of free Governments, and as they become incorporated with the national sentiment, counteract the impulses of interest and passion."[38]

Congressional legislation and executive orders—especially those that result from campaign promises—typically are also fairly visible. Perhaps the greatest difficulty, especially in the area of congressional legislation, is a result of complexity. Both because Congress is itself organized in such a complex fashion (with, for example, a host of committees and subcommittees) and because legislation requires concurrence of both houses and either presidential approval and/or a congressional override, the public may find it more difficult to "track" such actions than the amending process. Similarly, because laws sometimes take up literally hundreds of pages and embody countless compromises—many made behind closed doors—the public may not be in a good position to understand the details of such legislation.

Judicial decisions are arguably even less visible. Not only do courts frequently write such decisions in arcane legalistic language, but frequently such decisions are fairly fact specific. As a rule, the public devotes less attention to such decisions than to either amendments and/or legislation or executive orders.

When times are extraordinary and issues are highly visible, however, changes in constitutional interpretation by the Courts may follow a period of so much deliberation and attention that the change is as visible, or almost as visible, as if the nation had ratified an amendment. Scholars may fret that there is no archaeological evidence for the Court's so-called switch in time that saved nine in the text of the Constitution itself, but contemporaries could hardly claim that change had been effected secretly. The Court gave more than adequate signals of what it was doing.[39] Especially over time, the attention devoted to such Supreme Court decisions as those dealing with racial desegregation, prayer in schools, and abortion suggests that, in this respect at least, the switch-in-time case was far from a category of one.

STABILITY

Arguably, alterations effected through all three mechanisms of change are relatively stable, but changes effected by constitutional amendment are considerably more stable than those effected by the elected branches or through judicial interpretation. Whereas only amendments can directly overturn other amendments, both amendments and other more readily effected laws and executive orders may overturn other laws and executive orders. While there are thus many examples of laws and executive orders which have overturned previous laws and executive orders and judicial decisions which have reversed prior judicial decisions, only one constitutional amendment has specifically repealed another, and this repeal took fourteen years and considerable public experience and debate.[40] Thus, a writer comparing the Sherman Act with the Commerce Clause noted that the former, having been adopted by constitutional mechanisms is equally law of the land with the latter but that the latter "has what insurance companies would call a better expectation of life." Elaborating, he noted that "owing to the obstacles placed in the way of its repeal[,] it has a greater chance of longevity."[41] Moreover, writers sometimes lament the fact that some important legal changes were not incorporated into the Constitution and are hence not as stable as they might otherwise be. A commentator on the Court's switch during the New Deal thus notes that "proponents of a more expansive view [of federal responsibility over social welfare] can point to a half century of federal practice and judicial approval but no specific constitutional sanction. Without explicit constitutional defense, the New Deal's legislative heritage rests on sand."[42]

Somewhat complicating this picture is the fact that there are numerous judicial decisions at both the state and federal level which have seemingly thwarted or reversed changes effected through constitutional amendment in the short term. The Court's early treatment of the Fourteenth Amendment and the states' posture toward the Fifteenth Amendment are but two prominent examples.[43] Both of these examples might also suggest, however, that written words embodied in the text of the Constitution are surprisingly resilient over time. Certainly, some of the impetus for *Brown v. Board of Education*'s reversal of *Plessy v. Ferguson* was the continuing force of the Equal Protection Clause, however muted these words had sometimes been over the previous century.[44]

FLEXIBILITY

Flexibility is the flip side of stability, and there are certainly advantages to leaving some matters to the discretion of future generations.[45] Scholars sometimes praise the U.S. Constitution for its brevity and favorably contrast it to state constitutions in this respect. Such scholars would likely argue that it is better to initiate changes through legislation that can later be reversed than it is to freeze changes in the Constitution or in judicial interpretations thereof.

The key, of course, is to decide which objects of government are permanent and which are not. Few contemporary Americans would probably be comfortable allowing the rights designated in the first ten amendments to rest simply on judicial whim. In the terminology of the American Framers, it is necessary to distinguish between those rights which are natural and unchanging and those which are not.[46] To the extent that laws, executive orders, and judicially initiated changes involving matters other than natural rights can be more easily reversed than can amendments, such changes would appear to have the advantage.[47]

To the extent that both constitutional amendments and judicial decisions "constitutionalize" matters, however, the above caution might be a better argument for refusing to allow some issues (alcoholic prohibition is perhaps the classic case; balanced budget proposals may be another)[48] to be translated into the constitutional dimension by either constitutional amendment or judicial decision.[49] Justice Holmes, for one, believed that the Constitution not only did not, but also should not, sanction one economic theory over another.[50] Similarly, H. Jefferson Powell argues in a recent book that one advantage of preferring "majoritarian decision making" to "judicial activism" is that the former has an "endlessly *revisable* character," whereas the latter "is a language of permanence, of settled decision, of absolute political value. Matters subject to judicial decision in the name of the Constitution are, by definition, beyond ordinary revision, perhaps beyond legitimate revision altogether."[51]

DEMOCRACY

Because the American Founders did not advocate direct, or pure, but representative democracy,[52] no institution in America can unequivocally claim to speak for the people per se. Arguably, the two elected branches come closest to reflecting the popular will. Given a president who does not use his veto power, a majority of both houses of Congress can thus adopt legislation by a simple majority.

In comparing changes effected by judicial interpretation and those brought about by constitutional amendment, it is apparent that neither is an especially democratic process. To begin with the amending process, instead of a direct vote or referendum by the people, it requires votes within Congress and the state legislatures.[53] Given these majorities, it is extremely unlikely that amendments could be adopted which would be directly contrary to the will of the people. Because both of these votes require supermajorities (two-thirds votes of both houses of Congress and ratifications by three-fourths of the states), however, there may be many changes which a simple numerical majority favor which are not and may never become part of the U.S. Constitution.[54] Jane Mansbridge notes the difficulty when she observes that:

> the framers of the Constitution meant to give intense, sizable minorities a near veto on constitutional amendments, and they succeeded.

This raises a democratic paradox. We sometimes think of the rights-oriented amendments to the Constitution as having the function of protecting politically disadvantaged groups from the power of the majority. Yet the Constitution requires much more than a majority to pass these amendments.[55]

Advocates of judicial activism are likely to be most vocal in such cases. Should the nation be bound by the dead hand of the past, by anachronistic interpretations of the Constitution, when public opinion has clearly progressed and become more enlightened?[56] Shouldn't the Constitution grow with the times? At this point, proponents of judicial activism advocate democracy, and such advocates can make a particularly powerful argument for judicially effected changes in cases like legislative malapportionment where the normal democratic processes might be blocked or stymied.[57] On such occasions, the Court simply does not act as the counter-majoritarian institution some have portrayed it to be.[58]

On the other hand, while judicial initiatives may coincide with democratic sentiments, judicial initiatives neither require majorities at the state nor at the congressional level.[59] Hence, the judicial branch may initiate or reverse changes without even majority support, much less the kind of strength required to adopt constitutional amendments. While judicial review thus has the power to initiate changes favored by a majority that is less than that required to muster two-thirds of both Houses of Congress and three-fourths of the states, it may also initiate changes not favored even by a numerical majority.[60] Moreover, Cass Sunstein has argued that "reliance on the courts may impair democratic channels for seeking change, and in two ways. It might direct energy and resources from politics, and the eventual judicial decision may foreclose a political outcome."[61] Similarly, referring to "the decay of citizenship and a decline in popular government," Hickok and McDowell note that "a society that relies upon courts and judges to make the important political and moral decisions is a society that has lost touch with what self-government is about. It is a society in which citizenship has little or no meaning."[62]

There are few better examples of the possible tensions between popular sentiment and judicial decisions than the death penalty cases in which Justice Thurgood Marshall first argued that the penalty "was morally unacceptable to the people of the United States at this time in their history"[63] and subsequently extended on his earlier view that the Court's duty to enhance human dignity required it to follow the mandate, not of the citizenry as a whole, but of that part of the citizenry who were most informed and enlightened.[64] Were the Court to declare the death penalty to be unconstitutional per se, as both Brennan and Marshall consistently urged it to do,[65] only the Supreme Court itself or a constitutional amendment requiring congressional and state majorities could reverse the decision. Here, then, is a counter-majoritarian difficulty. The ability of the courts to further majority ideals which cannot be translated into constitutional amendments is balanced by the judiciary's capacity to thwart majority will in decisions which are rarely reversed by such amendments.

PROTECTION OF MINORITY RIGHTS

The American system balances majority rule against respect for minority rights, and advocates of judicial review often cite the protection of minority rights as a key duty of, and justification for, judicial review.[66] Amendments, decisions by the political branches, and judicial decisions have all expanded, and/or formalized, the rights of minorities. Laws and judicial decisions have, however, sometimes restricted such rights as well. As the product of elected representatives, laws and executive orders are particularly susceptible to pressure from the majority to enhance their own rights at the expense of the rights of others. Two authors thus citing congressional laws against Communists and subversives in the period after World War II contend that "Congress was so responsive to, and partly the cause of, ill-reasoned public opinion that it was a poor guardian of political rights."[67] Although such amendments have been proposed, no amendment (with the possible exception of the Eighteenth which was subsequently repealed) has ever restricted minority rights. There are some notable court decisions which have done so.[68] More typically, minorities look to the courts for protections which majorities might not be willing to extend to them. At least since Justice Stone formulated the *Carolene Products* Footnote, the Court has been particularly solicitous of such rights.[69]

SUSCEPTIBILITY TO SPECIAL INTERESTS

Almost from the time that the Framers expressed concern about the influence of factions,[70] Americans have looked suspiciously on the possibility that governmental actions will reflect the pressures of special interests rather than the common good.[71] As with a number of other measures utilized in this chapter, there is no ready comparison of the effects of special interests on each of the methods of change discussed here, but one can hazard some general observations.

Interest group pressures have certainly often fueled the amending process. To cite but two related instances, the Anti-Saloon League helped to secure the adoption of the Eighteenth Amendment, and the Voluntary Committee of Lawyers helped repeal it.[72] Given the visibility that typically surrounds the amending process, as well as the majorities required at both stages of this process, it is difficult to muster the special interests securing an amendment without wider majority support, except in those presumably rare instances where such interests might be advantaged by the federal nature of the system. The emphasis of the amending process on consensus, however, practically guarantees an important role for dedicated majorities opposed to amendments, and the history of the Equal Rights Amendment is an example where such organization by committed interest groups proved successful.[73]

Certainly, as a bicameral body with an elaborate committee and subcommittee system, Congress provides multiple leverage points for special interests. Thus, one study has concluded that American public policy is generally "more responsive to special interests than to general interests,"[74] and another argues that "the adoption of key statutes generally follows the application of substantial pressure from interest groups, often abetted by public opinion."[75] Fund-raising pressures on both congressional and presidential candidates also give special access to those interest groups with money.

On the surface, changes instituted by the courts should be relatively free of the direct influence of special interests, and, indeed, some scholars have justified judicial solicitude for certain rights precisely on the basis that such attention helps provide a counterweight to the ability of such powerful interest groups to influence the political branches.[76] There are mechanisms, for example, the *amicus curiae* brief, through which special interests do have input into judicial decision making, but, according to one study, "it is common for the Supreme Court to reach a major decision for which significant interest group and public support are lacking."[77]

FEDERALISM

Both the legislative process and the amending process represent state interests.[78] In the legislative process, the adoption of the Seventeenth Amendment may have somewhat weakened this commitment,[79] but not only are representatives still elected from districts within the states, but the Constitution still guarantees each state an equal voice in the Senate. Moreover, unlike certain parliamentary democracies which have significantly curtained the power of the upper house, the U.S. Constitution still requires Senate concurrence for the adoption of all legislation.[80] Similarly, the amending process is structured so as to reflect federal concerns.[81] When it comes to ratification of such amendments, states are represented as states. Whatever popular majorities may favor an amendment, it can only be ratified if three-quarters of the states approve.[82] As Lester B. Orfield has observed: "There is one type of situation where prima facie it seems that a minority is sovereign in the United States. A minority of the states may block an amendment. A single state may defeat the abolition of the equal suffrage clause."[83] Federal representation within Congress and the amending process have not, of course, kept either institution from mandating some changes—national alcoholic prohibition, for example—whose advocates had little apparent concern for state or regional differences.

Given the supremacy clause, judicially initiated changes require no such state approval. Certainly, there are justices—some of whom, like Justice O'Connor, have participated in state politics—who are sensitive to federal concerns,[84] but the Supreme Court is not structured so that justices consider themselves to be representatives of the states. Thus, some scholars have criticized certain decisions of the Supreme Court—its abortion rulings, for example—because the Court imposed a single nationwide rule where state variation might have been more appropriate,[85] and, on some occasions, justices have indicated that they accord less deference to state actions than to actions by the other two branches of the national government.[86]

To say that the legislative and amending processes are more federal in nature does not in and of itself, of course, indicate whether they are therefore a better or worse means of effecting change. Those who think that state concerns need special attention will certainly be more likely to favor the legislative and amending processes while those who view federalism as an obstacle to change or as inherently undemocratic might well favor judicially initiated changes precisely for those reasons.

SEPARATION OF POWERS

Although the U.S. Constitution does not specifically mention separation of powers, the organization of the document into separate articles—the first three of which establish the legislative, executive, and judicial powers—certainly indicate the Framers' commitment to this idea.[87] Of the three methods of constitutional change discussed in this book, the legislative path is probably the most likely to reflect separation of powers concerns in that such legislation is subject both to a presidential veto and to subsequent judicial review. Similarly, executive orders may be modified by subsequent legislation and/or be declared unconstitutional by the judicial branch.

Currently, the amending process does not directly reflect separation of powers concerns. Arguably, amendments are more likely to be proposed by two-thirds majorities in both houses of Congress and to be subsequently ratified if they have presidential support, but the president is not required to sign such amendments,[88] and, while courts certainly have to interpret amendments in cases properly before them, the justices have generally insisted that they will second-guess neither the constitutionality of such amendments[89] nor the procedural questions surrounding them.[90]

Changes initiated by the judicial branch may be energized by the other two branches, and the cooperation of these two branches might on occasion be essential for their implementation, but neither of the other two branches is needed for the formulation of such changes. Moreover, whereas amendments proposed by Congress require subsequent ratification by the states, judicial decisions require no such direct appeal.

Walter Murphy has sagely remarked that the Constitution does not "create a network of shared powers at the national level so that citizens can take to the street celebrating a trifurcated institutional system";[91] rather, this design was instituted to protect liberty. To the extent that judicial mechanisms for effecting change are more unchecked by the doctrine of separated powers, there is greater danger for such a threat, although different individuals would obviously assess the threat differently.[92]

PERCEIVED LEGITIMACY

This book is premised on the belief that constitutional amendments, congressional legislation and executive orders, and judicial interpretations are all accepted methods of constitutional change in certain circumstances. Given the role of the courts in deciding on the constitutionality of laws and executive orders, there are clearly perceived limits beyond which legislative and executive mechanisms cannot go and maintain their legitimacy.

Because of the ambiguity involved in whether the judicial task is primarily that of interpretation or adaptation, however, scholars sometimes critique the Court for usurping the amending function,[93] particularly when it relies for authority on ambiguous language. Arguably, the Court's central authority comes from its focus on constitutional interpretation rather than on its capacity for initiating constitutional change per se.[94]

Largely because constitutional amendments require the mobilization of supermajorities, once ratified, they are less subject to attack than a process that requires a simple majority of votes on the Supreme Court.[95] Supreme Court decisions are routinely criticized in a way that amendments typically are not.

HISTORICAL AND TEXTUAL SUPPORT

Given 200 years of experience with the amending process, the legislative process, and judicial review, all are fairly well-established mechanisms of constitutional change. As discussed above, however, the broad role of the legislative and executive authorities is necessarily circumscribed the closer they come to matters related to the Constitution.

In comparing the processes of constitutional amendment and judicial review, the former is certainly better justified from a textual point of view than is the latter, and scholars and dissenting justices frequently critique broad judicial decisions on the basis that the changes are so extensive that they can only be justified by amendment. Thus, in the *First Income Tax Case*, Justice White said that "if it was necessary that the previous decisions of this Court should be repudiated, the power to amend the Constitution existed and should have been availed of,"[96] while in the *Second Income Tax Case*, Justice Harlan said that the previous cases upholding the income tax should not have been voided "*without an amendment of the constitution.*"[97] In *Home Building and Loan Association v. Blaisdell* (1934), Justice Sutherland argued that "constitutions can not be changed by events alone. They remain binding as the acts of the people until they are amended or abrogated by the action prescribed by the authority which created them."[98] In an even more classic statement, Justice Black noted in the *Griswold* Decision that amendment was preferable to judicial construction, the former method being both "good enough for our Fathers" and "good enough for me."[99] Similarly, in *Harper v. Virginia State Board of Elections* (1966), Black argued that "when a 'political theory' embodied in our Constitution becomes outdated, it seems to me that a majority of the nine members of this Court are not only without constitutional power but are far less qualified to choose a new constitutional political theory than the people of this country proceeding in the manner provided by Article V."[100]

If the text commends resort to the amending process, numerous other constitutional institutions and practices—including judicial review itself— are also based on necessary implication. Moreover, from the Court's early history through its last session, it has inaugurated literally hundreds of changes in constitutional interpretation, and it is a bit late in the constitutional day to argue that all such measures have been ill advised or unconstitutional. While one must move hesitatingly from the "is" of constitutional history to the "ought" of constitutional theory, a theory divorced from history will certainly be inadequate.

A reading of American history might suggest principles by which one could argue that one or another mechanism for change is more appropriate in initiating some changes than for others. Ely's argument that judicially initiated changes are particularly appropriate in cases where the normal democratic processes are blocked has already been mentioned.[101] One might further suggest that judicial decisions sanctioning changes already agreed to by other branches and more generally by popular mandate—the New Deal for example—are more appropriate than changes without such a consensus behind them.[102]

On the negative side, there are especially good reasons for the courts to hesitate to reverse changes already initiated by amendment or to forestall changes about to be so initiated. Similarly, one might hypothesize that the courts should be more reluctant to institute major changes than small ones. One might also distinguish between judicial actions in cases of constitutional silence as opposed to cases of constitutional sanction or prohibition. Beyond such theoretical generalizations and prudential admonitions, it is difficult to go.

SAFETY AND REGULARITY

It is important that mechanisms designed to bring about constitutional change be well understood and that the processes of change do not themselves result in unanticipated negative consequences.[103] In this writer's judgment, no existing mechanism for peaceful change is in and of itself dangerous, although it is certainly possible to imagine proposed changes that might be so radical that they would bring about considerably more harm than good.

Although the regularity of the post–Civil War amendments and the Twenty-Seventh Amendment was questionable (as were the attempts to ratify the proposed Child Labor Amendment and to extend the ratification deadline for the proposed Equal Rights Amendment),[104] most amendments have been adopted with relative regularity. Some still debate whether the Congress or the Court should be the ultimate arbiter of questions surrounding this process,[105] but, to date at least, such debates have never resulted in a standoff where one branch accepted an amendment that another did not.

Periodically, commentators have expressed fears about the safety of the constitutional convention mechanism. In one of the better-reasoned, albeit sharply worded, pieces of this sort, Laurence Tribe argued that such a convention would risk "three distinctive confrontations of nightmarish dimension—confrontations between Congress and the Convention, between Congress and the Supreme Court, and between the Supreme Court and the states."[106] While no mechanism is completely fail-safe, the author believes that Paul Weber and Barbara Perry have established that there are adequate "political 'safety latches' " in place which make such scenarios quite unlikely.[107]

One can imagine one or another of the three branches of government creating a danger by attempting to push through changes that the others thought to be inappropriately instituted short of amendment, but ordinarily one would expect that the natural institutional rivalry (treated in this chapter under the heading "Separation of Powers") would be sufficient to discourage this. The formal amending process itself ultimately stands as a kind of popular guardian against dangerous changes instituted by the three branches.

CONSTITUTIONAL PROLIXITY AND STYLE

Part of the beauty of the U.S. Constitution is its compactness.[108] Accordingly, scholars often praise the document over more prolix state constitutions where even minor governmental changes often require constitutional emendations,[109] or with complex laws and judicial interpretations with their increasingly complex formulae.[110] In addition to taking up more shelf space, an overly precise Constitution tends unduly to tie the hands of the current generation.

As was indicated under the earlier discussion of constitutional flexibility, however, the warning against excessive amendments might also serve as a warning against judicial "constitutionalizing" of issues which might be better left to the elected branches of government.

CLARITY

James Madison once noted the inherent ambiguity of all communications involving words,[111] and amendments, laws and orders, and judicial decisions all share in this limitation. By their nature, constitutional amendments are more succinct and accessible than all but the most curt of court orders and laws, but, as the history of the Ninth and Fourteenth Amendments and arguments over the proposed Equal Rights Amendment aptly demonstrate, amendments are not necessarily any clearer on that account. While there are no concurring or dissenting opinions to record when amendments are adopted, debates over their scope and meaning may sometimes fulfill a similar obfuscating function. In theory at least, a court opinion binds only the direct parties to a case and is restricted to the specific circumstances raised in that proceeding; laws, orders, and amendments apply more broadly to all who fall within their purview.

While amendments generally get the nod for clarity, then, there are nonetheless times when a series of Supreme Court decisions might well serve a similar "clarifying" or "translating" function,[112] as, for example, the numerous cases since 1937 in which the Court has repudiated substantive due process in economic affairs or affirmed the civil rights of African-Americans and other minorities. The Court's repetitive citation of past cases further aids its communicative function.[113] While a single law or amendment is likely to send a clearer message than a solitary court decision, this edge in clarity might well give way when one compares a single amendment or law to a long-standing series of court decisions, especially if these decisions received a lot of publicity or generated heated controversy.

UNITY

Related to clarity is unity. One sometimes overlooked advantage of effecting a change through a constitutional amendment is that, once ratified, such an amendment generally speaks in a unified voice. This unity may be somewhat undercut both by the fact that some amendments might embody principles in tension or in conflict (as in the case of the Fourteenth Amendment which arguably attempted both to preserve minority rights and to preserve the federal system) and by the fact that those who favor rival interpretations of amendments sometimes attempt to read differing interpretations into the record of congressional debates. The typical brevity of amendments, like those of some executive orders, especially when compared to the prolixity of corresponding laws, is generally likely to lead to greater clarity.

In early American history, decisions of the Supreme Court followed English custom and allowed justices to author their own opinions, but John Marshall abandoned this procedure when he became chief justice.[114] While dissents were thus relatively rare in the Marshall years, justices have written "literally thousands" of them in the years that have followed.[115] There are certainly occasions where the judicial branch also speaks in a unified voice—the Supreme Court's unanimous repudiation of segregation in *Brown v. Board of Education* (1954),[116] its rebuke to Governor Faubus in *Cooper v. Aaron*,[117] and its eight-to-zero rejection of Nixon's claims of executive privilege in *United States v. Nixon*[118] constitute three striking examples.

Frequently, however, the opinion for the Court is accompanied by concurring or dissenting opinions which might serve to muddle its message and give hope to those who disfavor it, especially in close cases. The *Bakke Case* certainly serves as a classic example, with four justices arguing against all uses of racial classifications, four willing both to permit such classifications and to accept racial quotas in this case, and a single justice (Lewis Powell) left with the Solomonic role of declaring some benign uses of race permissible but deciding that, at least under the circumstances in that case, quotas were unacceptable.[119]

Some recent decisions have been even more convoluted. Consider, for example, the summary of the Court's opinion in *Arizona v. Fulminante* (1991):

> WHITE, J., delivering an opinion, Parts I, II, and IV of which are for the Court, and filed a dissenting opinion in Part III. MARSHALL, BLACKMUN, and STEVENS, JJ., joined Parts I and II; and KENNEDY, J., joined parts I and IV. REHNQUIST, C. J., delivered an opinion, Part II of which is for the Court, and filed a dissenting opinion in Parts I and III. O'CONNOR, J., joined Parts I, II, and III of that opinion; KENNEDY and SOUTER, JJ., joined Parts I and II; and SCALIA, J., joined Parts II and III. KENNEDY, J., filed an opinion concurring in the judgment.[120]

To the extent that such mixed messages reach the public—and dissenting opinions are especially written with a desire to gain such attention—they certainly impede implementation of the majority view.

DELIBERATION

One of the advantages promoted by the relative difficulty of the amending process is that measures are unlikely to be incorporated into the fundamental law without due "deliberation and consideration."[121] The presence of both a congressional forum and additional arenas in each of the states with the attendant publicity likely to surround each assures this. The necessary congressional and state majorities simply cannot propose and ratify amendments by accident; on this point, at least, the familiar path marked out by the Article V mechanism appears to be almost fail-safe.[122]

The legislative process also involves considerable deliberation, requiring, as it does, concurrence of both houses and either presidential approval or an override by a supermajority. The pressures of popular opinion may sometimes undermine such deliberation by influencing representatives interested in re-election to put greater stress on passing laws than on seeing that such laws are constitutional.

If the amending process requires deliberation in multiple forums and likely over a period of some months or years, and the legislative process usually requires similar consensus, the judicial system also promotes deliberation. Before courts will render judgments, two parties with genuine adversarial interests must first present the courts with a legitimate "case or controversy."[123] Each party has the opportunity to present its case both orally and through written briefs; interested outside parties frequently supplement such arguments with *amicus curiae* briefs.[124] Moreover, the Supreme Court generally will decide cases dealing with major constitutional issues only after such issues have been thoroughly aired in the lower courts. Such a venting of the issues, like the written opinion of the Court itself and its attendant publicity, will typically call attention to any departures from past precedents, and the media, if not the general public, often waits upon the judicial determination of major decisions much as it might wait upon the outcome of a proposed amendment.

RESPECT FOR THE CONSTITUTION

Paul Freund has observed that "a constitution is both a code to be obeyed and a symbol to be venerated."[125] To the extent that age and the appearance of stability enhance such veneration, there might be dangers if the formal processes of amendment are used too frequently. In Freund's words, "Proliferating amendments would impair the sense of attachment to the old and familiar, the spirit of loyal devotion to a deeply rooted institution."[126] Freund aptly cited Madison's critique of Jefferson's proposals for more frequent constitutional alterations.[127] Among Madison's responses was his argument that "as every appeal to the people would carry an implication of some defect in the government, frequent appeals would, in great measure, deprive the government of that veneration which time bestows on everything, and without which perhaps the wisest and freest governments would not possess the requisite stability."[128]

Freund suggests that interpretation is one way of balancing the need for change against the popular desire for stability.[129] There is, however, always the possibility that major shifts in interpretation by the judicial and/or the elected branches will have a similar effect. Certainly, one argument for *stare decisis* has been the argument that to abandon the principle is to undermine respect for the Court. Undoubtedly, the people expect the three branches of government to initiate changes consistent with existing constitutional language, but, should these branches go too far, this might itself undermine respect for the constitutional system.

CONSTITUTIONAL ATROPHY

Critics of judicial activism have long argued that overreliance on the courts saps the democratic process by transferring decisions that should be made by the people to an elitist, and essentially undemocratic, institution.[130] As one writer puts it: "A society that for too long deflects to an unelected institution its responsibilities to act upon its principles ultimately risks losing its ability to engage in responsible normative debate."[131] In a similar vein, some contemporary constitutional scholars argue that excessive reliance on the judicial branch to effect constitutional changes will result in the atrophy both of popular participation in government and of the written Constitution itself. They fear that the written Constitution could become little more than an archaeological relic, or talisman, more revered than heeded.[132] For them, for the judiciary to institute most changes in constitutional interpretation and/or to "constitutionalize" most contemporary issues is, in fact, to trivialize the written Constitution and to make it but a mouthpiece for the current occupants of the Supreme Court rather than the fundamental law it was intended to be.[133] Such critics argue that Article V would not have been made part of the Constitution if the Founders anticipated widespread use of other methods of constitutional change.

Other scholars who put greater emphasis on the "spirit" than the "letter" of the Constitution argue that the Constitution's central strength is its articulation of fundamental values,[134] its statement of constitutional aspirations,[135] and/or its fragmented distribution of governmental powers.[136] For proponents of such emphases, vigorous judicial enforcement of an ever-widening concept of human dignity is not the atrophying of the Founders' ideals but their true flowering. Those emphasizing the role of the Constitution in distributing governmental powers point to continuing skirmishes between the judicial branch and the other two as signs that the constitutional order is still healthy and that the written Constitution is still vigorous. For them, Article V is simply too big a gun to direct against most constitutional problems when other means are available with their own constitutional safeguards.

EFFICACY

Certainly, any serious proponent of change will seek assurance that changes occur not only in law but also in reality. For a number of years now, scholars have cautioned that Supreme Court decisions are not as effective as might be anticipated.[137] In examining the role of the judiciary in the American system, Henry Abraham thus concludes that *"The Court may have the last say, but potentially it has the last say only for a time."*[138] In a recent study examining the efficacy of social changes initiated by the courts, Gerald Rosenberg has redirected attention to three constraints that courts face in implementing social changes. These limitations include "the limited nature of constitutional rights, the lack of [judicial] independence, and the judiciary's lack of powers of implementation."[139] Rosenberg indicates that the first constraint can be overcome when "there is ample precedent for change," the second, when there is "support for change from substantial numbers in Congress and from the executive," and the third, when "there is either support from some citizens, or at least low levels of opposition from all citizens" and where one of four other conditions is present.[140]

In examining the issues of civil rights, abortion, women's rights, the environment, reapportionment, and criminal law, Rosenberg concluded that Courts have been much less effective in implementing changes than most scholars have heretofore thought. In concluding his survey, Rosenberg argues that in those cases where court actions appear to have been most effective, their contribution is often "akin to officially recognizing an evolving state of affairs, more like the cutting of the ribbon on a new project than its construction."[141] In an even more shocking analogy, Rosenberg argues that "courts act as 'fly-paper' for social reformers who succumb to the 'lure of litigation.' "[142] While Rosenberg's analysis is not necessarily the final word on the subject, it certainly calls into question the effectiveness of judicial reforms, especially those that do not have solid support by the other two branches of government.[143]

This chapter, of course, addresses a comparative question, and some of the issue areas that Rosenberg addressed were not the sole responsibility of the judiciary. While this author knows of no comparable study of the effectiveness of constitutional amendments, some amendments have certainly proved to be ineffective, especially in the short run. When the Bill of Rights was first suggested, James Madison was among those who expressed doubts about the value and efficacy of such a "parchment barrier,"[144] and experience has subsequently demonstrated that "constitutional provisions are not self executing."[145] While the Thirteenth Amendment put a relatively quick end to the remnants of slavery, the attempts by the Fourteenth and Fifteenth Amendments to guarantee equal citizenship rights and equal voting rights to African-Americans were strikingly ineffective for almost 100 years. The Prohibition Amendment and the laws passed to enforce it, while not without some impact,[146] were notorious for the opposition and evasion they spawned in the years before the Twenty-First Amendment repealed the Eighteenth. Amendments guaranteeing voting rights to women and eighteen years olds, by contrast, were almost immediately effective.

Scholars have generally treated the implementation of legislative and judicial policies separately,[147] but, as in the case of judicial decisions, there is often a gap between the promise of legislation and its subsequent implementation.[148] Moreover, those comparative studies which do exist suggest that the legislative branch generally has the advantage over the judicial branch in implementing its own policies.[149]

To the extent that amendments, like other forms of law, rely for their implementation on popular and/or institutional support and on widespread knowledge of the law, the required majorities for proposal and ratification of amendments should typically assure that such knowledge and support would be available. In this regard, one might note that ratification of the post–Civil War amendments, which were so evaded, was in large part a result of requiring ratification by southern states as a condition to renewed representation within Congress[150] and that a sitting president had adamantly opposed at least one of these amendments—the Fourteenth.[151] It is also clear that there was built-in tension within the Fourteenth Amendment between a commitment to fundamental rights and a continuing commitment to federalism.[152] The federal dimension of the amending process may also have played a more important part in the proposal and ratification of the Prohibition Amendment—which deeply split many urban and rural areas—than in other amendments,[153] thus not necessarily assuring that the amendment had majority popular support.[154]

Proponents of amendments that require a long-term commitment to changes in personal behavior might also find that support by the public and/or by the political branches, lags over time.[155] Such reflections would suggest that, especially over the long haul, neither judicial decisions, nor laws and executive orders, nor constitutional amendments will be particularly successful in implementing policies which have little support in, and are not directly approved by, popular opinion.

FINALITY

Law and executive orders lack finality both because subsequent congresses or presidents can repeal them and because the judgment of their constitutionality is subject to judicial review. While the amending process and the process of judicial review are in constant tension, each capable of influencing the other, there is reason for according a certain finality to constitutional amendment which is not present when it comes to judicial interpretations. The issue is not simply that judicial decisions may alter with changes in personnel and other attempts at regulating judicial jurisdiction,[156] but also that amendments ultimately have power to "trump" judicial interpretations. Thus, in comparing constitutional amendments to other types of change, one writer has noted that "if any question of conflict should arise, formal amendment is of greater significance than the others because it can override any of the others. Whatever changes may be brought about through the other processes, formal amendment can reverse them all."[157] Moreover, should the Court "misinterpret" an amendment, the people could always adopt another amendment clarifying their intentions.[158] Thus, the amending process is appropriately recognized as "the ultimate authority in the state and the one within whose ambit all others must operate."[159]

The priority of the formal amending powers' authority is implicit in a Constitution grounded on "We the people of the United States." That is, this formal process is the one designated for the people to express their sovereignty in concrete nonrevolutionary form.[160]

TYPES OF CHANGE

Sanford Levinson's analysis which was cited in the previous chapter suggests that some changes are too minor to be considered true "amendments" (even when formally incorporated into the Constitution through use of the Article V process), while other changes are conceivably so radical that they too would not be considered to be mere "amendments."[161] While this author hesitates to follow Levinson in expanding or contracting the term *amendment* from its very precise legal meaning—and hence prefers either Lutz's more clearcut distinction between constitutional *amendment* and constitutional *revision*,[162] or Munzer and Nickel's distinction between formal and informal amendment[163]—Levinson's analysis is certainly quite useful in pointing to the fact that not all constitutional changes are created equal. Moreover, the importance of a legal change is not necessarily indicated by whether or not it has or has not been officially added to the written Constitution through Article V processes.

One can plausibly argue, however, that certain of the mechanisms of change discussed in this book are more appropriately utilized for certain kinds of changes than for others. To take a situation that is undoubtedly easier to state than to apply, one might be extremely uncomfortable living in a system professing adherence to a written Constitution and yet permitting the three branches of government to initiate changes counter to the language, the original intentions, the contemporary understandings, and all other generally accepted interpretative principles, especially in cases where all these standards were congruent and were relatively unambiguous. Thus, it is difficult to imagine changing the terms of the president or members of Congress, making the position of Supreme Court justices elective, abolishing freedom of speech or religion, or reinstituting slavery absent an Article V amendment or even a completely different Constitution. By the same token, in cases where the text of the Constitution, the understanding or original intent, contemporary understandings and other generally accepted interpretative principles are all permissive—for example, in deciding on the precise contours of the application of the exclusionary rule or on deciding precisely when a search warrant is or is not necessary—the Article V amending process might seem to be a relatively big gun to aim at the problem, unless, of course, the public is attempting to finalize a rule or understanding contrary to existing governmental practice.

More generally, one can argue that the more important the change, the greater the rationale there is for use of Article V processes. To return to Levinson's terminology, Article V processes would be most appropriate for amendments, whereas mere interpretations would not require such heavy constitutional artillery. One obvious difficulty with what is otherwise a plausible normative principle is that the principle has not always been followed in historical practice. As Levinson has himself pointed out, many Article V amendments have not, under his scheme of classification, been true amendments. Perhaps more importantly for the analysis here, the nation effected one of the three central "constitutional moments" that Bruce Ackerman has identified—namely, the New Deal—without the use of any such Article V processes. The varied indices cited in this chapter should show that this does not mean that this change was therefore illegitimate, but they suggest that following a path that bypassed Article V carried some distinct negative costs.

ADEQUACY

How, then, does one assess the adequacy of the three processes of change? This may largely depend on whether one considers the processes singly or together. Viewed either in terms of the number of times it has been successfully utilized or in comparison with the processes of other nations, there is certainly reason to believe that the current process of formal amendment is too difficult.[164] Similarly, critics often argue that the exercise of judicial review has been too active and too little subject to restraint,[165] and others have criticized the political system for being in gridlock. All such critiques must be balanced both by acknowledging that the Framers intended for the Constitution to put certain obstacles in the way of popular democracy and that there are times—the New Deal, Lyndon Johnson's Great Society, and, to a lesser extent, Ronald Reagan's first term in office—where ordinary obstacles no longer appear to be all that formidable.

As indicated in the opening chapter of this book, one of the central objectives that the Founding Fathers sought in formulating an amending process was to avoid future resort to violent revolution. No such violent revolutions have occurred since 1776 unless one counts the Civil War. Not only was this war partly precipitated by an attempt to read the Constitution in too restrictive a fashion,[166] but the Constitution was criticized at the time for being too rigid.[167] Somewhat ironically, one of the Southerner's fears, dating at least as far back as the writings of John C. Calhoun,[168] was that the existing mechanism would not provide sufficient protection for slavery if the northern states decided to eliminate it.[169]

Throughout American history, criticisms of both the formal amending process and of the judiciary have waxed and waned. Three amendments followed relatively quickly upon the critiques of the amending process that preceded the Civil War, while a series of four amendments followed critiques early in the Progressive Era.[170] On four occasions, the nation adopted amendments to reverse Supreme Court decisions with at least two amendments (the Fourteenth and Sixteenth) following periods of judicial activism. As mentioned above, periods of relatively quick change have followed periods of constitutional gridlock. Such events suggest, but do not prove, that current processes for change are generally capable of responding to increasing public pressure for such changes but that these processes often resist such pressures in the short run.

INTERACTION

If, as the thesis of this book suggests, the three mechanisms for change constantly interact, then the use, disuse, or perceived misuse of any one mechanism will undoubtedly affect the other two. Regular resort to one mechanism for change might thus contribute to the disuse of, or prompt resort to, the others, just as the difficulty of one mechanism might make resort to the other two more likely.

In thus addressing the process of constitutional amendment and what he calls judicial "revision," Donald Lutz has hypothesized—as have others before him—that one of the reasons that judicial revisions of the Constitution have become so commonplace is that the formal Article V process is so difficult.[171] Similarly, if, as Ackerman has documented, the three branches of government are intent on initiating change, Article V amendments may prove largely unnecessary. Alternatively, if the public believes that the ordinary political processes are not adequately responding to public sentiments, they may use the Article V process (and especially the still untried convention mechanism) to initiate changes on their own. If the people believe that political processes are instituting changes too frequently, they may exercise either their votes or the Article V process to halt or reverse such changes. Thus, Gary L. McDowell argues that the increasing number of single-issue amendments that have been proposed in Congress are largely "a frustrated response to an increasingly active judiciary whose opinions no longer seem to have any connection with the theory of limited republican government embraced by the Constitution."[172]

It is therefore clear that the relationship among the three processes of change described in this book is dynamic and potentially synergistic. One of the insights of Bruce Ackerman's work is that he has indicated that, especially in the case of major changes, such alterations are likely to reflect more than the simple operation of a formalistic process and that they may even avoid the process altogether. The analysis in this chapter is directed to indicating that each method of change comes with a unique blend of costs and benefits, some of which are manifest in the short term and others over the long haul.

SUMMARY

In comparing constitutional changes effected by constitutional amendments with those initiated by laws or orders and those effected by judicial interpretations, then, there are a whole range of relevant issues. These are illustrated in Figure 6.1, which conveniently summarizes the material presented in this chapter.

Constitutional Amendments	Judicial Interpretations	Laws and Orders
CONSTITUTIONAL ATROPHY		
Put priority on letter and writtenness of Constitution	More likely to emphasize spirit of Constitution and articulation of basic values	Involve elected officials
EFFICACY		
Efficacy varies; adoption process usually guarantees popular and institutional support	Efficacy varies; judicial fiat does not assure popular and institutional support	Law making process generally guarantees popular and institutional support
FINALITY		
Have power to reverse judicial decisions	Have power to interpret amendments; may be weakened by political branches	Subject to judicial review and legislative or executive repeal
TYPES OF CHANGE		
Appropriate for major changes and for changes counter to language of existing Constitution	Especially appropriate for minor changes not contrary to, and arguably implicit in, or growing out of existing document	Especially appropriate for minor changes not addressed in the existing document
ADEQUACY		
27 successes, several after intense criticism of process	Many exercises, some reviewing other court decisions	Periods of activity follow periods of gridlock
INTERACTION		
Difficult amending process makes other types of change more likely	May prompt or preempt the need for amendment or actions by the elected branches	May prompt or preempt the need for amendment or judicial decisions

Figure 6.1
Methods of Change in Comparative Perspective

Constitutional Amendments	Judicial Interpretations	Laws and Orders
SAFETY AND REGULARITY		
Generally quite safe. Some questions about convention mechanism	Checked by other branches and Article V	Checked by other branches and Article V
CONSTITUTIONAL PROLIXITY AND STYLE		
Add to constitutional prolixity	Do not add to prolixity of Constitution but have similar effect	Do not add to prolixity but have similar effect
CLARITY		
Usually sends clear message	Message most clear if there is series of cases	Clarity variable
UNITY		
Speak with single voice; debates may reflect ambiguity	Sometimes unanimous. Often accompanied by concurrences and dissents	Prolixity may lead to varied interpretations
DELIBERATION		
Require deliberations at national and state level	Require deliberation in single branch	Require deliberation in single branch
RESPECT FOR THE CONSTITUTION		
Undermined by too frequent change	Could be weakened if went too far	Could be weakened if went too far

Figure 6.1
Methods of Change in Comparative Perspective (continued)

Constitutional Amendments	Judicial Interpretations	Laws and Orders
DEMOCRACY		
Require supermajorities to enact or repeal	Can be initiated or reversed without majorities or supermajorities	Require legislative majorities
PROTECTION OF MINORITY RIGHTS		
Unlikely to restrict rights	More likely to expand or restrict rights	More likely to expand or restrict rights
SUSCEPTIBILITY TO SPECIAL INTERESTS		
Likely to prod broader publics. Might stop amendments favored by public	Costs of litigation may favor well-funded interests. *Amicus curiae* briefs possible	Multiple access points and need for funds may lead to influence
FEDERALISM		
Federal concerns built into the process	Sensitivity to federal concerns more variable	Some federal concerns built into process
SEPARATION OF POWERS		
Aided by help from the president but do not require it	Can be initiated, but not always sustained, without support from other two branches	Generally require legislative/executive cooperation
PERCEIVED LEGITIMACY		
Legitimacy widely recognized	Legitimacy more likely to be questioned	Legitimacy depends on whether areas are considered within constitutional parameters
HISTORICAL AND TEXTUAL SUPPORT		
Strong textual support	Strong support in historical practice and implication	Textual and historical support will vary by issue

Figure 6.1
Methods of Change in Comparative Perspective (continued)

	Constitutional Amendments	Judicial Interpretations	Laws and Orders
EASE			
	Especially difficult to enact	Difficulty varies according to court majority	Difficult but somewhat variable
RANGE			
	Subject to one stated limit	Limited by text and by self-imposed notions of interpretation	Limited by popular oversight and judicial review
SPEED			
	Typically slow: can be speeded	Highly variable: depends on current majority	Highly variable
DIRECTION			
	Typically into the unknown	Typically affirm the status quo; periods of innovation followed by periods of consolidation	Typically into the unknown but within constitutional restraints
VISIBILITY			
	Highly visible	Visibility more variable but enhanced by a series of decisions	Fairly visible but sometimes complex
STABILITY			
	Highly stable	Stability varies	Can be repealed, rescinded, or declared unconstitutional
FLEXIBILITY			
	Fairly inflexible	Flexibility variable	Flexibility variable

Figure 6.1
Methods of Change in Comparative Perspective (continued)

IMPLICATIONS FOR POLICY MAKERS

This author realizes that, in the end, proponents and opponents of constitutional change will more likely choose their strategy on the basis of what is more likely to result in what they consider to be favorable policy outcomes than on the basis of abstract constitutional considerations. On the one hand, those who believe they need but a new law or executive order or another vote on the Supreme Court to usher in changes they desire and who further doubt whether they can muster public opinion behind them are hardly likely to expend the energy to work for a constitutional amendment. Those who know, on the other hand, that the Court is now against them and is likely to be so in the foreseeable future while believing they have a clear majority of public opinion behind them may think that they have little option but to press for a constitutional amendment.

The existence of such a choice is a tribute to the dynamic tension of the American constitutional system. To focus exclusively on immediate concerns about which route is most likely to result in victory for one's side is, however, to ignore the link between individual policy issues and larger matters of constitutional interpretation. If the author has succeeded in bringing these matters into clearer focus, he will think that his book has been worth writing.

NOTES

1. The author hopes the dimensions he has chosen are fairly exhaustive, and he has attempted to focus on dimensions which illuminate all sides of the issue, but he would especially welcome suggestions as to additional dimensions that he might find it useful to consider.

After writing this chapter, the author realized that Lester B. Orfield had analyzed amendments, albeit not rival mechanisms of constitutional change, along five dimensions—federalism, wisdom and efficiency, deliberation, popular democracy, clarity and certainty, and enforcement. See Orfield's, *The Amending of the Federal Constitution* (Ann Arbor: University of Michigan Press, 1942), pp. 206–21.

2. The former rather than the latter requirement has been the most formidable. Of thirty-three amendments proposed by the necessary majorities of Congress, twenty-six or twenty-seven have been subsequently ratified by the states.

3. Donald S. Lutz argues that a low amendment rate in a long-standing document like that in the United States "strongly implies the use of some alternate means of revision to supplement the formal amendment process." See "Toward a

Theory of Constitutional Amendment," paper presented at the American Political Science Convention, Chicago, Illinois, September 1992, p. 40.

4. Richard B. Bernstein with Jerome Agel, *Amending America: If We Love the Constitution So Much, Why Do We Keep Trying to Change It?* (New York: Times Books, 1993), p. 175.

5. David R. Mayhew, *Divided We Govern: Party Control, Lawmaking, and Investigations, 1946–1990* (New Haven, CT: Yale University Press, 1991).

6. As discussions from a previous chapter should indicate, Justices who feel especially bound by precedent might be reluctant to overturn decisions even with which they disagree for fear of jeopardizing the stability of the law or the perceived legitimacy of judicial judgments.

7. *Planned Parenthood v. Casey*, 112 S. Ct. 2791 (1992). Michael J. Gerhardt thus notes that "the last thing one would have expected the Rehnquist Court to do was to reaffirm *Roe v. Wade*." See "The Pressure of Precedent: A Critique of the Conservative Approaches to *Stare Decisis* in Abortion Cases," *Constitutional Commentary* 10 (Winter 1993), p. 67.

8. One reason Franklin Roosevelt apparently waited so long to try to pack the Court was that, in view of the unanimous decision against him in *Schechter Poultry Corp. v. United States*, 295 U.S. 495 (1935), he did not initially believe that adding new members would still give him a majority. See William E. Leuchtenburg, "The Origins of Franklin D. Roosevelt's 'Court-Packing' Plan," *The Supreme Court Review*, ed. Philip B. Kurland (Chicago: University of Chicago Press, 1966), p. 361.

9. This was the concern demonstrated earlier in the *Casey Case*, footnote 7 *supra*.

10. Jefferson thus wrote to Wilson Cary Nicholaus: "I had rather ask an enlargement of power from the nation, where it is found necessary, than to assume it by a construction which would make our powers boundless. Our peculiar security is in the possession of a written Constitution. Let us not make it a blank paper by construction." Quoted by Henry Adams, *The Formative Years: A History of the United States During the Administration of Jefferson and Madison*, vol. 2, ed. Herbert Agar (London: Collins, 1948), p. 185.

11.. Thus, the last clause of Article V provides that states may not be deprived of equal suffrage in the Senate without their consent.

12. This topic is treated extensively in John R. Vile, *Contemporary Questions Surrounding the Constitutional Amending Process* (Westport, CT: Praeger, 1993), pp. 127–54.

13. It is interesting that while some such amendments have been proposed (e.g., the Bricker Amendment of the 1950s), no amendment has ever been ratified which relates primarily to matters of foreign policy.

14. The best-known collection of such proposals is still probably Herman Ames's, *The Proposed Amendments of the Constitution of the United States During the First Century of Its History* (New York: Burt Franklin, 1970; reprint of 1896 edition). For reference to subsequent collections, see Vile, *Contemporary*

Questions, note 113, pp. 21–22. For one additional work, see Daryl B. Harris, *Proposed Amendments to the U.S. Constitution: 99th–101st Congresses (1985–1990)*, (Washington, DC: Congressional Research Service, July 9, 1992).

15. *United States v. Carolene Products Company*, 304 U.S. 149 (1938).

16. Bernstein with Agel, *Amending America*, p. 155.

17. For a useful survey of current debates, see Philip Bobbitt, "Constitutional Interpretation," *The Oxford Companion to the Supreme Court of the United States*, ed. Kermit L. Hall (New York: Oxford University Press, 1992), pp. 183–90. Also useful is *Interpreting the Constitution: The Debate Over Original Intent*, ed. Jack N. Rakove (Boston: Northeastern University Press, 1990).

18. Ronald Dworkin refers to such specific provisions as "conceptions" rather than "concepts." See *Taking Rights Seriously* (Cambridge, MA: Harvard University Press, 1977), pp. 134–36.

19. Henry J. Abraham, *The Judicial Process*, 6th ed. (New York: Oxford University Press, 1993), pp. 347–73.

20. Thus, although Article I, Section 9, provides for "a regular Statement and Account of the Receipts and Expenditures of all public Money," the Supreme Court denied standing to those in *United States v. Richardson* who challenged the secrecy of the budget for the CIA and other intelligence-gathering agencies. See 418 U.S. 166 (1974).

21. See Richard Neustadt, *Presidential Power: The Politics of Leadership* (New York: John Wiley and Sons, 1960).

22. The best-known work in this area is still probably *The Impact of Supreme Court Decisions*, 2d ed., ed. Theodore J. Becker and Malcolm M. Feeley (New York: Oxford University Press, 1973).

23. Alexander Hamilton, James Madison, and John Jay, *The Federalist Papers*, intro. by Clinton Rossiter (New York: New American Library, 1961), p. 465. *Federalist* No. 78.

24. For a study which argues that congressional initiatives are often more progressive than presidential actions, see Gary Orfield, *Congressional Power: Congress and Social Change* (New York: Harcourt Brace Jovanovich, 1975), pp. 257–58, p. 322. On p. 325, Orfield notes that Congress "has the power to take decisive action" but that a majority of its members "rarely believe the public demands such change."

25. "The Anatomy of Constitutional Revolutions," *Nebraska Law Review* 68 (1989), pp. 701–806.

26. For the most extensive breakdown of all the steps involved in the regularized amending procedure, see Denys P. Myers, *The Process of Constitutional Amendment*, Senate Document No. 314, 76th Congress, 3d Session, 1940, especially, pp. 2–9.

27. The author of an analysis of congressional statutory overrides of Supreme Court decisions found that "almost half . . . were overridden within two years of their decision (ten were overridden the year they were decided), two-thirds were overridden within five years, and three-fourths within ten years." See William N.

Eskridge, Jr., "Overriding Supreme Court Statutory Interpretation Decisions," *The Yale Law Journal* 101 (November 1991), p. 345.

28. Alan P. Grimes, *Democracy and the Amendments to the Constitution* (Lexington, MA: Lexington Books, 1978), p. 147.

29. See chart in William S. Livingston, *Federalism and Constitutional Change* (Oxford: The Clarendon Press, 1956), p. 230.

30. This amendment is discussed at greater length in chapter 1 of this book.

31. Grimes, p. 75, notes that Andrew Johnson "had been an early proponent of direct election of the Senate."

32. This amendment was first proposed in Congress in 1869. See Clement Vose, *Constitutional Change: Amendment Politics and Supreme Court Litigation Since 1900* (Lexington, MA: Lexington Books, 1972), p. 47.

33. Some commentators have upheld this extension by distinguishing between limits within the texts of amendments and those which are found in the authorizing resolutions that accompany them. See, for example, Walter Dellinger, "The Legitimacy of Constitutional Change: Rethinking the Amending Process," *Harvard Law Review* 97 (1983), p. 425. On this whole issue, see Vile, *Contemporary Questions*, pp. 45–54.

34. See Richard Kluger, *Simple Justice*, 2 vols. (New York: Alfred A. Knopf, 1975).

35. Anthony Lewis, *Gideon's Trumpet* (New York: Vintage Books, 1964).

36. One problem with the Twenty-Seventh Amendment was that, while it had been on the table for 200 years, many people seemed unaware that it was about to be adopted. Hence, this author once dubbed this the stealth amendment. See John R. Vile, "Just Say No to 'Stealth' Amendment," *The National Law Journal* 14 (June 22, 1992), pp. 15–16.

37. Thus, comparing formal constitutional amendments to cambrian rings, William Van Alstyne has argued that court decisions rarely have such status: "Famous case names are *not* cambrian rings. They are at best rabbinical annotations on a dead sea scroll. *Reed v. Reed*, for instance, has no equivalent status as the ill-fated Equal Rights Amendment would have possessed." See Van Alstyne's "Notes on a Bicentennial Constitution: Part I, Processes of Change," *University of Illinois Law Review* (1984), p. 935. *Reed v. Reed*, to which Van Alstyne refers, dealt with whether men should be automatically preferred to women in the administration of a child's estate. See 404 U.S. 71 (1971).

38. Letter from Madison to Jefferson dated 17 October 1788. Cited in Alpheus T. Mason and Donald G. Stephenson, Jr., *American Constitutional Law*, 10th ed. (Englewood Cliffs, NJ: Prentice-Hall, 1993), p. 350.

39. Bruce Ackerman argues that the Court's opposition to the New Deal prior to 1937 served a *"signalling function,"* which "made it abundantly plain to the mass of private citizens that a fundamental constitutional initiative was being seriously entertained by their representatives in the nation's capital." See "The Storrs Lectures: Discovering the Constitution." *The Yale Law Journal* 93 (May 1984), p. 1054.

40. Clement Vose, *Constitutional Change*, pp. 101–39.

41. Herbert W. Horwill, *The Usages of the American Constitution* (Port Washington, NY: Kennikat Press, 1969; reprint of 1925), p. 19. Donald J. Boudreaux and A. C. Pritchard make a similar point in "Rewriting the Constitution: An Economic Analysis of the Constitutional Amendment Process," *Fordham Law Review* 62 (October 1993), p. 112.

42. David E. Kyvig, "The Road Not Taken: FDR, the Supreme Court, and Constitutional Amendment," *Political Science Quarterly* 104 (Fall 1989), p. 481.

43. Both are discussed in the first chapter of this book.

44. Van Alstyne, "Notes on a Bicentennial Constitution," p. 957, however, attributes some of the reluctance to ratify amendments to the fear that they will come to have "uncertain careers" at the hands of judicial interpreters.

45. Indeed, Thomas Jefferson frequently suggested that constitutions should be changed each generation, that is, approximately every nineteen years. For Jefferson's views, see John R. Vile, *The Constitutional Amending Process in American Political Thought* (New York: Praeger, 1992), pp. 63–66.

46. Thomas Jefferson thus observed that "nothing . . . is unchangeable but the inherent and unalienable rights of man." See Vile, *The Constitutional Amending Process in American Political Thought*, p. 61.

47. Summarizing the view (which he does not share) of those who favor judicial innovation rather than the use of Article V, Van Alstyne, "Notes on a Bicentennial Constitution," p. 950, notes that "the Court process is far superior to the formal amendment process in this regard, moreover, because in so far as later events may be persuasive that a particular constitutional innovation by the Court was not as well-advised as circumstances originally suggested, the quasi-amendment may be retracted in the same process that called it into being; neither the innovation nor its elimination is subjected to the heavy machinery of article V."

48. "The Balanced Budget Amendment: An Inquiry Into Appropriateness," *Harvard Law Review* 96 (May 1983), p. 1600.

49. The Framers of the American Constitution were very cognizant of the need to keep matters that would be subject to frequent change out of the document. See Philip A. Hamburger, "The Constitution's Accommodation of Social Change," *Michigan Law Review* 88 (November 1989), pp. 239–327.

50. In his dissenting opinion in *Lochner v. New York* (1905) Holmes thus noted that "a constitution is not intended to embody a particular economic theory, whether of paternalism and the organic relation of the citizen to the state or of laissez-faire." 198 U.S. 45, 75.

Mary Ann Glendon's, *Rights Talk: The Impoverishment of Political Discourse* (New York: The Free Press, 1991) suggests that the language of rights often precludes sensible compromise. Her work might thus serve as a further warning against constitutionalizing matters which might better be left to the political process.

51. H. Jefferson Powell, *The Moral Tradition of American Constitutionalism: A Theological Interpretation* (Durham, NC: Duke University Press, 1993), p. 298.

Powell cites the conflict over the constitutionality of the proposed flag-burning amendment in explanation of the last phrase of his quotation.

52. *The Federalist Papers*, pp. 81–83.

53. Indeed, in *Hawke v. Smith* (No. 1), 253 U.S. 221 (1920), the Supreme Court declared unconstitutional a state constitutional provision which mandated approval of amendments through popular referenda.

54. In examining results of survey research, Austin Ranney discovered that "substantial majorities of the general public have favored nine of the eleven" proposals he examined. These included "ERA, balanced budgets, school prayers, direct election of presidents, regional presidential primaries, a national presidential primary, national initiative, limiting terms of senators and representatives, and presidential item veto." Needless to say, none of these have become amendments. See "What Constitutional Changes Do Americans Want?," in American Political Science Association and American Historical Association, *This Constitution: Our Enduring Legacy* (Washington, DC: Congressional Quarterly, 1986), p. 285.

55. Jane J. Mansbridge, *Why We Lost the ERA* (Chicago: University of Chicago Press, 1986), p. 34.

56. Thomas C. Grey notes that a pure interpretive model of judicial review would probably have to reject the "prevailing view that the eighth amendment's prohibition of cruel and unusual punishments must be 'interpreted' in light of society's 'evolving standards of decency.' " See "Do We Have an Unwritten Constitution?" *Stanford Law Review* 27 (February 1975), p. 713.

57. The most compelling case has probably been made by John H. Ely in *Democracy and Distrust* (Cambridge, MA: Harvard University Press, 1980).

58. The term *counter-majoritarian* is most frequently associated with Alexander M. Bickel, *The Least Dangerous Branch: The Supreme Court at the Bar of Politics*, 2d ed. (New Haven, CT: Yale University Press, 1986), pp. 16–23.

59. Arguably, one can make a stronger case for judicial recognition of embracive acts of legislation initiated by the political branches than for judicial initiation of change. Thomas Peebles argues that a fundamental change occurred in American constitutional law when the judicial branch began utilizing the idea of an organic Constitution for "striking down rather than sustaining legislation." See "A Call to High Debate: The Organic Constitution in Its Formative Era, 1840–1920," *University of Colorado Law Review* 52 (Fall 1980), p. 103.

60. Here, then, the Court does act in a counter-majoritarian fashion. Bickel, *The Least Dangerous Branch*, pp. 16–23.

61. Cass R. Sunstein, *The Partial Constitution* (Cambridge, MA: Harvard University Press, 1993), p. 145.

62. Eugene W. Hickok and Gary L. McDowell, *Justice vs. Law: Courts and Politics in American Society* (New York: The Free Press, 1993), p. 219.

63. *Furman v. Georgia*, 408 U.S. 238, 360 (1978).

64. *Gregg v. Georgia*, 428 U.S. 153, 231–41, especially pp. 232–33, (1976).

65. For Brennan's view, see William J. Brennan, Jr., "The Constitution of the United States: Contemporary Ratification," *South Texas Law Review* 27 (Fall 1985), p. 443.

66. See, for example, Michael J. Perry, *The Constitution, the Courts and Human Rights* (New Haven, CT: Yale University Press, 1982).

67. Stephen R. Munzer and James W. Nickel, "Does the Constitution Mean What It Always Meant?" *Columbia Law Review* 77 (November 1977), pp. 1060–61.

68. See, for example, *Dred Scott v. Sandford*, 60 U.S. 393 (1857) and *Korematsu v. United States*, 323 U.S. 214 (1944). For further examples, see Louis Fisher, "One of the Guardians, Some of the Time," in *Is The Supreme Court the Guardian of the Constitution?* ed. Robert A. Licht (Washington, DC: AEI Press, 1993), pp. 87–91.

69. *United States v. Carolene Products Company*, 304 U.S. 144 (1938).

70. James Madison in *Federalist* No. 10 in Hamilton, Madison, and Jay, *The Federalist Papers*.

71. This attitude was reflected in the negative view many of the Framers had toward political parties. See Richard Hofstader, *The Idea of a Party System: The Rise of Legitimate Opposition in the United States, 1780–1840* (Berkeley: University of California Press, 1972).

72. Vose, *Constitutional Change*, pp. 69–137.

73. Bernstein with Agel, *Amending America*, pp. 142–43.

74. Randall B. Ripley and Grace A. Franklin, *Congress, the Bureaucracy, and Public Policy*, 5th ed. (Pacific Grove, CA: Brooks/Cole Publishing Company, 1991), p. 182.

75. Lawrence Baum, "Comparing the Implementation of Legislative and Judicial Policies," in *Implementation and Public Policy*, ed. Daniel A. Mazmanian and Paul A. Sabatier (Lexington, MA: Lexington Books, 1981), p. 42.

76. Henry J. Abraham, *The Judiciary: The Supreme Court in the Governmental Process,* 8th ed. (Dubuque, IA: Wm C Brown, 1991), p. 91.

77. Baum, "Comparing the Implementation," p. 42.

78. The electoral college—the mechanism by which presidents are formally elected—also embodies federal concerns. Proponents of this mechanism often cite this federal dimension as an argument for its continuation.

79. See chapter 2 of this book for details.

80. Thus, in overturning *National League of Cities v. Usery*, 426 U.S. 833 (1976), and in choosing not to exempt state public transportation from provisions of the Fair Labor Standards Act, Justice Blackmun noted in *Garcia v. San Antonio Metropolitan Transit Authority*, 469 U.S. 528 (1985), that state interests were adequately protected by their representation in Congress. Some find confirmation of this fact in the subsequent congressional decision to allow state and local governments to substitute compensatory time off in place of overtime pay. For this development, see Ralph A. Rossum and G. Alan Tarr, *American Constitu-*

tional Law: Cases and Interpretation, 3d ed. (New York: St. Martin's Press, 1991), p. 217.

81. Walter Dellinger, "The Amending Process in Canada and the United States: A Contemporary Perspective," *Law and Contemporary Problems* 45 (Autumn 1982), p. 288.

82. For concern about the impact of the federal features of the amending process on democracy, see Peter Suber, "Population Changes and Constitutional Amendments: Federalism versus Democracy," *Journal of Law Reform* 20 (Winter 1987), pp. 409–90.

83. *The Amending of the Federal Constitution* (Ann Arbor: University of Michigan Press, 1992), p. 159.

84. Beverly B. Cook, "Justice Sandra Day O'Connor: Transition to a Republican Court Agenda," *The Burger Court: Political and Judicial Profiles*, ed. Charles M. Lamb and Stephen C. Halpern (Urbana: University of Illinois Press, 1991), pp. 250–52.

85. Markman, "The Jurisprudence of Constitutional Amendments," p. 91.

Markman's criticism seems overly broad. There certainly are decisions in which the Court has been somewhat sensitive to state and local variations. The Court's obscenity ruling in *Miller v. California* [413 U.S. 15 (1973)] incorporating the idea of contemporary community standards is a good example.

86. See the Court's discussion of the "political questions" doctrine in *Baker v. Carr*, 369 U.S. 186 (1962).

87. For explication of this principle see James Madison in Hamilton, Madison and Jay, *The Federalist Papers*, No. 51.

88. This principle was established in the case of *Hollingsworth v. Virginia*, 3 U.S. 379 (1798).

89. *National Prohibition Cases*, 253 U.S. 350 (1920).

90. *Coleman v. Miller*, 307 U.S. 433 (1939). This criticism has, however, been subject to a good deal of criticism. See chapter 2 of Vile, *Contemporary Questions*.

91. "An Ordering of Constitutional Values," *Southern California Law Review* 53 (January 1980), p. 749.

92. In critiquing judicial changes for bypassing the separation of powers, Markman, "The Jurisprudence of Constitutional Amendments," pp. 91–92, puts primary emphasis on the way that bypassing separation of powers, judicially effected changes tend to lack the benefits of compromise.

93. See, for example, Stephen J. Markman, "The Amendment Process of Article V: A Microcosm of the Constitution," *Harvard Journal of Law & Public Policy* 12 (1989), pp. 117–18.

94. See Van Alstyne, "Notes on a Bicentennial Constitution," p. 948, for a comparison of the Founders' views of constitutional change versus those of modern judicial activists.

95. This is one reason that procedural regularity is so important to the formal amending process. Part of the initial weakness of the post–Civil War amend-

ments may well have stemmed from the ambiguity that surrounded their processes of ratification wherein southern states were required to ratify as a recondition to congressional representation in Congress.

96. *Pollock v. Farmers' Loan & Trust Co.*, 157 U.S. 429, 639 (1895).

97. *Pollock v. Farmers' Loan & Trust Co.*, 158 U.S. 601, 672 (1895).

98. 290 U.S. 389, 451 (1934).

99. 381 U.S. 479, 522 (1965).

100. 383 U.S. 663, 678 (1966).

101. Ely, *Democracy and Distrust*.

102. Ackerman, p. 1056.

103. Walter Dellinger thus notes that "a satisfactory amendment process demands, at a minimum, that the rules for the adoption of an amendment be clearly understood." See "The Legitimacy of Constitutional Change: Rethinking the Amendment Process," *Harvard Law Review* 97 (December 1983), p. 387.

104. See Vile, *Contemporary Questions*, pp. 45–54.

105. These questions are treated in Vile, *Contemporary Questions*, chapter 2.

106. "Issues Raised by Requesting Congress to Call a Constitutional Convention to Propose a Balanced Budget Amendment," *Pacific Law Journal* 10 (1979), pp. 634–35.

107. *Unfounded Fears: Myths and Realities of a Constitutional Convention* (New York: Praeger, 1989), p. 105. Also see Vile, *Contemporary Questions*, chapter 4.

108. Notes written by Randolph for the Committee of Detail at the Constitutional Convention thus indicate the Committee's desire when drafting the Constitution "to insert essential principles only, lest the operations of government should be clogged by rendering those provisions permanent and unalterable, which ought to be accommodated to times and events and to use simple and precise language, and general propositions." See *The Records of the Federal Convention of 1787*, ed. Max Farrand (New Haven, CT: Yale University Press, 1966), p. 137.

109. Malcolm R. Eiselen, "Dare We Call a Federal Convention?" *The North American Review* 244 (1937), pp. 35–36. Donald S. Lutz, "Toward a Theory of Constitutional Amendment," paper presented at the American Political Science Convention, Chicago, Illinois, September 1992, p. 11, posits that "the longer a constitution the higher its amendment rate, and the shorter a constitution the lower its amendment rate."

110. See Robert F. Nagel's comparison of the free speech and commerce clauses of the Constitution with court-inspired alternatives in *Constitutional Cultures: The Mentality and Consequences of Judicial Review* (Berkeley: University of California Press, 1989), pp. 126–27. Nagel suggests, p. 128, that the current judicial style "is an amalgam of the bureaucratic and the academic."

111. Hamilton, Madison, and Jay, *Federalist* No. 37, p. 229.

112. The term is Ackerman's, *We the People*, p. 1054.

113. Martin Shapiro, "Toward a Theory of Stare Decisis," *Courts, Judges and Politics*, 4th ed., ed. Walter F. Murphy and C. Herman Pritchett (New York: Random House, 1986), pp. 427–30.

114. Donald E. Lively, *Foreshadows of the Law: Supreme Court Dissents and Constitutional Development* (Westport, CT: Praeger, 1992), pp. xxii and xxiv–v.

115. Ibid., p. xxiv.

116. 347 U.S. 483 (1954). The importance that Chief Justice Earl Warren placed on achieving a unanimous verdict in this case is aptly documented in Kluger, *Simple Justice*, vol. 2, pp. 830–83.

117. 358 U.S. 1 (1958). In this historic case, the name of each justice was placed at the head of the case to indicate the Court's unity.

118. 418 U.S. 683 (1974). As a former member of the Department of Justice, William Rehnquist recused himself from this case.

119. *Regents of the University of California v. Bakke*, 438 U.S. 265 (1977).

120. 111 S. Ct. 1246 (1991) as cited in Joseph Goldstein, *The Intelligible Constitution* (New York: Oxford University Press, 1992), p. xi.

121. This terminology is from the Supreme Court's decision in *Hawke v. Smith*, (No. 1) 253 U.S. 221, 226 (1920).

122. There is, of course, some concern about the untried convention mechanism for proposing amendments. This author believes that such fears are largely unjustified. See Vile, *Contemporary Questions*, pp. 55–74.

123. Abraham, *The Judicial Process*, pp. 373–78.

124. Ibid., p. 253, notes that there were 120 briefs filed in the historic *Bakke Case*.

125. Paul A. Freund, "To Amend—or Not to Amend the Constitution," *New York Times Magazine* (December 13, 1964), p. 33.

126. Ibid., p. 117.

127. Madison's and Jefferson's views on the subject are analyzed at greater length in Vile, *The Constitutional Amending Process in American Political Thought*, pp. 36–38 and 63–67.

128. Hamilton, Madison, and Jay, *The Federalist Papers*, p. 314.

129. "To Amend—or Not to Amend the Constitution," p. 117.

130. In such a vein, Justice Frankfurter explained his opinion in the *Flag Salute Cases* in a memorandum to Justice Harlan dated May 27, 1940: "For my intention was to use this opinion as a vehicle for preaching the true democratic faith of not relying on the Court for the impossible task of assuring a vigorous, mature, self-protecting and tolerable democracy by bringing the responsibility for a combination of firmness and toleration directly home where it belongs—to the people and their representatives themselves." See Mason and Beaney, *American Constitutional Law*, p. 615.

131. Frederick A. O. Schwarz, Jr., "The Constitution Outside the Courts," *Cardozo Law Review* 14 (April 1993), p. 1292.

132. Thomas E. Brennan, "Return to Philadelphia," *Cooley Law Review* 1 (1982), pp. 21–29.

133. Van Alstyne, "Notes on a Bicentennial Constitution," pp. 947–51.

134. Brennan, "The Constitution of the United States: Contemporary Ratification," pp. 433–45.

135. Sotorious A. Barber, *On What the Constitution Means* (Baltimore, MD: Johns Hopkins University Press, 1984).

136. Davis, "Constitutional Change Through Judicial Review: A Dialectical View."

137. Theodore L. Becker and Malcolm M. Feeley, eds., *The Impact of Supreme Court Decisions*, 2d ed. (New York: Oxford University Press, 1973).

138. Abraham, *The Judiciary: The Supreme Court in the Governmental Process*, 6th ed. (Boston: Allyn and Bacon, 1983), pp. 185–86.

139. Rosenberg, *The Hollow Hope: Can Courts Bring About Social Change?* (Chicago: University of Chicago Press, 1991), p. 35.

140. Ibid., p. 36. These conditions are: "Positive incentives are offered to induce compliance, costs are imposed to induce compliance, court decisions allow for market implementation, or administrators and officials crucial for implementing are willing to act and see court orders as a tool for leveraging additional resources or for hiding behind."

141. Rosenberg, p. 338.

142. Ibid., p. 341.

143. For related critiques, see Jeremy Rabkin, *Judicial Compulsions: How Public Law Distorts Public Policy* (New York: Basic Books, 1989); R. Shep Melnick, *Regulation and the Courts: The Case of the Clean Air Act* (Washington, DC: The Brookings Institution, 1983); and Robert F. Nagel, *Constitutional Cultures*, especially pp. 27–59. Also useful is Thomas R. Marshall, "Policymaking and the Modern Court: When Do Supreme Court Rulings Prevail?" *Western Political Quarterly* 42 (December 1989), pp. 493–507, and Christopher E. Smith, *Courts and Public Policy* (Chicago: Nelson-Hall, 1993).

144. Bernstein with Agel, *Amending America*, p. 34.

145. Ibid., p. 269.

146. David E. Kyvig, ed., *Alcohol and Order: Perspectives on National Prohibition* (Westport, CT: Greenwood Press, 1985).

147. Baum, "Comparing the Implementation," p. 39.

148. See, for example, Jeffrey I. Pressman and Aaron Wildavsky, *Implementation*, 3d ed. (Berkeley: University of California Press, 1984) and Mazmanian and Sabatier's *Implementation and Public Policy*. For a more general discussion of the policy-making and implementing process, see Ripley and Franklin, *Congress, the Bureaucracy, and Public Policy*.

149. Baum, "Comparing the Implementation," p. 57.

150. The most thorough account of this controversy is found in Joseph B. James, *The Ratification of the Fourteenth Amendment* (Macon, GA: Mercer University Press, 1984).

151. Ackerman, *We the People*, p. 83.

152. William E. Nelson, *The Fourteenth Amendment: From Political Principle to Judicial Doctrine* (Cambridge, MA: Harvard University Press, 1988).

153. Grimes, *Democracy and the Amendments to the Constitution*, p. 86, thus notes that this argument was raised during congressional debates over this amendment.

154. Ibid., p. 109, notes that census prior to the apportionment of the Congress that proposed the Prohibition Amendment was "the last census in which the majority of Americans still lived in what were defined as rural areas."

155. To the extent that Prohibition was in part actuated by wartime sentiment, such sentiment could also be expected to lag over time. See Christopher N. May, *In the Name of War* (Cambridge, MA: Harvard University Press, 1989).

156. For congressional attempts to restrict judicial powers, see Walter F. Murphy, *Congress and the Court* (Chicago: University of Chicago Press, 1962); Stuart S. Nagel, "Court-Curbing Proposals in American History," *Vanderbilt Law Review* 18 (1965), pp. 925–44; and Edward Keynes with Randal K. Miller, *The Court vs. Congress: Prayer, Busing, and Abortion* (Durham, NC: Duke University Press, 1989).

157. Livingston, *Federalism and Constitutional Change*, p. 295.

158. Geoffrey R. Stone has, however, argued that "the Constitution of the United States should not be altered merely to 'correct' an 'erroneous' or 'unpopular' decision of the Supreme Court. Such a practice, once established as precedent, may prove too easy to follow and may lead, ultimately, to political and constitutional instability." Although Stone does not directly deal with the fact that four amendments have already "corrected" Supreme Court decisions, he seems especially concerned about alterations in the Bill of Rights. See Stone's, "In Opposition to the School Prayer Amendment," *The University of Chicago Law Review* 50 (Spring 1983), p. 842.

159. Livingston, *Federalism and Constitutional Change*, p. 295.

160. Lester B. Orfield, *The Amending of the Federal Constitution*, pp. 127–67. Also see Max Radin, "The Intermittent Sovereign," *Yale Law Journal* 39 (1930), p. 526.

161. "Accounting for Constitutional Change (Or, How Many Times Has the United States Constitution Been Amended? (A) <26; (B) 26; (C) > 26; (D) All of the Above)," *Constitutional Commentary* 8 (Summer 1991), p. 411.

162. Donald S. Lutz, "Toward a Theory of Constitutional Amendment," paper presented at the American Political Science Convention, Chicago, Illinois, September 1992, p. 6.

163. "Does the Constitution Mean What It Always Meant?" pp. 1045–46.

164. Lutz, "Toward a Theory of Constitutional Amendment," p. 39.

165. Markman, "The Amendment Process of Article V: A Microcosm of the Constitution," pp. 117–18.

166. See *Dred Scott v. Sandford*, 19 Howard (60 U.S.) 393 (1857).

167. See Sidney George Fisher's critique in chapter 6 of Vile, *The Constitutional Amending Process in American Political Thought*.

168. Ibid., pp. 87–88.

169. For a good discussion of attempts to avert the Civil War by amendment, see Bernstein with Agel, *Amending America*, pp. 71–93.

170. Vile, *The Constitutional Amending Process in American Political Thought*, pp. 137–56.

171. Ibid., pp. 40–41.

172. Gary L. McDowell, "On Meddling with the Constitution," *Journal of Contemporary Studies* 5 (Fall 1982), p. 11.

Appendix: The Amendments to the U.S. Constitution

AMENDMENTS TO THE CONSTITUTION OF THE UNITED STATES OF AMERICA

ARTICLES IN ADDITION TO, AND AMENDMENT OF, THE CONSTITUTION OF THE UNITED STATES OF AMERICA, PROPOSED BY CONGRESS, AND RATIFIED BY THE SEVERAL STATES, PURSUANT TO THE FIFTH ARTICLE OF THE ORIGINAL CONSTITUTION.

Amendment I.*

Congress shall make no law respecting an establishment of religion, or prohibiting the free exercise thereof; or abridging the freedom of speech, or of the press, or the right of the people peaceably to assemble, and to petition the Government for a redress of grievances.

Amendment II.

A well regulated Militia, being necessary to the security of a free State, the right of the people to keep and bear Arms, shall not be infringed.

Amendment III.

No Soldier shall, in time of peace be quartered in any house, without the consent of the Owner, nor in time of war, but in a manner to be prescribed by law.

*The first ten Amendments (Bill of Rights) were ratified effective December 15, 1791.

Amendment IV.

The right of the people to be secure in their persons, houses, papers, and effects, against unreasonable searches and seizures, shall not be violated, and no Warrants shall issue, but upon probable cause, supported by Oath or affirmation, and particularly describing the place to be searched, and the persons or things to be seized.

Amendment V.

No person shall be held to answer for a capital, or otherwise infamous crime, unless on a presentment or indictment of a Grand Jury, except in cases arising in the land or naval forces, or in the Militia, when in actual service in time of War or public danger; nor shall any person be subject for the same offence to be twice put in jeopardy of life or limb, nor shall be compelled in any criminal case to be a witness against himself, nor be deprived of life, liberty, or property, without due process of law; nor shall private property be taken for public use without just compensation.

Amendment VI.

In all criminal prosecutions, the accused shall enjoy the right to a speedy and public trial, by an impartial jury of the State and district wherein the crime shall have been committed; which district shall have been previously ascertained by law, and to be informed of the nature and cause of the accusation; to be confronted with the witnesses against him; to have compulsory process for obtaining witnesses in his favor, and to have the assistance of counsel for his defence.

Amendment VII.

In Suits at common law, where the value in controversy shall exceed twenty dollars, the right of trial by jury shall be preserved, and no fact tried by a jury shall be otherwise re-examined in any Court of the United States, than according to the rules of the common law.

Amendment VIII.

Excessive bail shall not be required, nor excessive fines imposed, nor cruel and unusual punishments inflicted.

Amendment IX.

The enumeration in the Constitution of certain rights shall not be construed to deny or disparage others retained by the people.

Amendment X.

The powers not delegated to the United States by the Constitution, nor prohibited by it to the States, are reserved to the States respectively, or to the people.

Amendment XI.*

The Judicial power of the United States shall not be construed to extend to any suit in law or equity, commenced or prosecuted against one of the United States by Citizens of another State, or by Citizens or Subjects of any Foreign State.

Amendment XII.**

The Electors shall meet in their respective states, and vote by ballot for President and Vice President, one of whom, at least, shall not be an inhabitant of the same state with themselves; they shall name in their ballots the person voted for as President, and in distinct ballots the person voted for as Vice-President, and they shall make distinct lists of all persons voted for as President, and of all persons voted for as Vice-President, and of the number of votes for each, which lists they shall sign and certify, and transmit sealed to the seat of the government of the United States, directed to the President of the Senate;—The President of the Senate shall, in the presence of the Senate and House of Representatives, open all the certificates and the votes shall then be counted;—The person having the greatest number of votes for President, shall be the President, if such number be a majority of the whole number of Electors appointed; and if no person have such majority, then from the persons having the highest numbers not exceeding three on the list of those voted for as President, the House of Representatives shall choose immediately, by ballot, the President. But in choosing the President, the votes shall be taken by states, the representation from each state having one vote;

a quorum for this purpose shall consist of a member or members from two-thirds of the states, and a majority of all the states shall be necessary to a choice. [And if the House of Representatives shall not choose a President whenever the right of choice shall devolve upon them, before the fourth day of March next following, then the Vice-President shall act as President, as in the case of the death or other constitutional disability of the President—-]† The person having the greatest number of votes as Vice-President, shall be the Vice-President, if such number be a majority of the whole number of Electors appointed, and if no person have a majority, then from the two highest numbers on the list, the Senate shall choose the Vice-President; a quorum for the purpose shall consist of two-thirds of the whole number of Senators, and a majority of the whole number shall be necessary to a choice. But no person constitutionally ineligible to the office of President shall be eligible to that of Vice-President of the United States.

Amendment XIII.*

Section 1. Neither slavery nor involuntary servitude, except as a punishment for crime whereof the party shall have been duly convicted, shall exist within the United States, or any place subject to their jurisdiction.

Section 2. Congress shall have power to enforce this article by appropriate legislation.

Amendment XIV.**

Section 1. All persons born or naturalized in the United States and subject to the jurisdiction thereof, are citizens of the United States and of the State wherein they reside. No State shall make or enforce any law which shall abridge the privileges or immunities of citizens of the United States; nor shall any State deprive any person of life, liberty, or property, without due process of law; nor deny to any person within its jurisdiction the equal protection of the laws.

Section 2. Representatives shall be apportioned among the several States according to their respective numbers, counting the whole number of persons in each State, excluding Indians not taxed. But when the right to vote at any election for the choice of electors for President and Vice President of the United States, Representatives in

*The Eleventh Amendment was ratified February 7, 1795.

**The Twelfth Amendment as ratified June 15, 1804.

†Superseded by section 3 of the Twentieth Amendment.

*The Thirteenth Amendment was ratified December 6, 1865.

**The Fourteenth Amendment was ratified July 9, 1868.

Congress, the Executive and Judicial officers of a State, or the members of the Legislature thereof, is denied to any of the male inhabitants of such State, being twenty-one years of age, and citizens of the United States, or in any way abridged, except for participation in rebellion, or other crime, the basis of representation therein shall be reduced in the proportion which the number of such male citizens shall bear to the whole number of male citizens twenty-one years of age in such State.

Section 3. No person shall be a Senator or Representative in Congress, or elector of President and Vice President, or hold any office, civil or military, under the United States, or under any State, who, having previously taken an oath, as a member of Congress, or as an officer of the United States, or as a member of any State legislature, or as an executive or judicial officer of any State, to support the Constitution of the United States, shall have engaged in insurrection or rebellion against the same, or given aid or comfort to the enemies thereof. But Congress may by a vote of two-thirds of each House, remove such disability.

Section 4. The validity of the public debt of the United States, authorized by law, including debts incurred for payment of pensions and bounties for services in suppressing insurrection or rebellion, shall not be questioned. But neither the United States nor any State shall assume or pay any debt or obligation incurred in aid of insurrection or rebellion against the United States, or any claim for the loss or emancipation of any slave; but all such debts, obligations and claims shall be held illegal and void.

Section 5. The Congress shall have power to enforce, by appropriate legislation, the provisions of this article.

Amendment XV.*

Section 1. The right of citizens of the United States to vote shall not be denied or abridged by the United States or by any State on account of race, color, or previous condition of servitude.

Section 2. The Congress shall have power to enforce this article by appropriate legislation.

Amendment XVI.**

The Congress shall have power to lay and collect taxes on incomes, from whatever source deriv-

*The Fifteenth Amendment was ratified February 3, 1870.
**The Sixteenth Amendment was ratified February 3, 1913.

ed, without apportionment among the several States, and without regard to any census or enumeration.

Amendment XVII.***

The Senate of the United States shall be composed of two Senators from each State, elected by the people thereof, for six years; and each Senator shall have one vote. The electors in each State shall have the qualifications requisite for electors of the most numerous branch of the State legislatures.

When vacancies happen in the representation of any State in the Senate, the executive authority of such State shall issue writs of election to fill such vacancies: *Provided*, That the legislature of any State may empower the executive thereof to make temporary appointments until the people fill the vacancies by election as the legislature may direct.

This amendment shall not be so construed as to affect the election or term of any Senator chosen before it becomes valid as part of the Constitution.

Amendment XVIII.†

[**Section 1.** After one year from the ratification of this article the manufacture, sale, or transportation of intoxicating liquors within, the importation thereof into, or the exportation thereof from the United States and all territory subject to the jurisdiction thereof for beverage purposes is hereby prohibited.

Section 2. The Congress and the several States shall have concurrent power to enforce this article by appropriate legislation.

Section 3. This article shall be inoperative unless it shall have been ratified as an amendment to the Constitution by the legislatures of the several States, as provided in the Constitution, within seven years from the date of the submission hereof to the States by the Congress.]

Amendment XIX.*

The right of citizens of the United States to vote shall not be denied or abridged by the United States or by any State on account of sex.

Congress shall have power to enforce this article by appropriate legislation.

***The Seventeenth Amendment was ratified April 8, 1913.
† The Eighteenth Amendment was ratified January 16, 1919. It was repealed by the Twenty-First Amendment, December 5, 1933.
*The Nineteenth Amendment was ratified August 18, 1920.

Amendment XX.**

Section 1. The terms of the President and Vice President shall end at noon on the 20th day of January, and the terms of Senators and Representatives at noon on the 3d day of January, of the years in which such terms would have ended if this article had not been ratified; and the terms of their successors shall then begin.

Section 2. The Congress shall assemble at least once in every year, and such meeting shall begin at noon on the 3d day of January, unless they shall by law appoint a different day.

Section 3. If, at the time fixed for the beginning of the term of the President, the President elect shall have died, the Vice President elect shall become President. If a President shall not have been chosen before the time fixed for the beginning of his term, or if the President elect shall have failed to qualify, then the Vice President elect shall act as President until a President shall have qualified; and the Congress may by law provide for the case wherein neither a President elect nor a Vice President elect shall have qualified, declaring who shall then act as President, or the manner in which one who is to act shall be selected, and such person shall act accordingly until a President or Vice President shall have qualified.

Section 4. The Congress may by law provide for the case of the death of any of the persons from whom the House of Representatives may choose a President whenever the right of choice shall have devolved upon them, and for the case of the death of any of the persons from whom the Senate may choose a Vice President whenever the right of choice shall have devolved upon them.

Section 5. Sections 1 and 2 shall take effect on the 15th day of October following the ratification of this article.

Section 6. This article shall be inoperative unless it shall have been ratified as an amendment to the Constitution by the legislatures of three-fourths of the several States within seven years from the date of its submission.

Amendment XXI.*

Section 1. The eighteenth article of amendment to the Constitution of the United States is hereby repealed.

Section 2. The transportation or importation into any State, Territory, or possession of the United States for delivery or use therein of intoxicating liquors, in violation of the laws thereof, is hereby prohibited.

Section 3. This article shall be inoperative

**The Twentieth Amendment was ratified January 23, 1933.

unless it shall have been ratified as an amendment to the Constitution by conventions in the several States, as provided in the Constitution, within seven years from the date of the submission hereof to the States by the Congress.

Amendment XXII**

Section 1. No person shall be elected to the office of the President more than twice, and no person who has held the office of President, or acted as President, for more than two years of a term to which some other person was elected President shall be elected to the office of the President more than once. But this Article shall not apply to any person holding the office of President when this Article was proposed by the Congress, and shall not prevent any person who may be holding the office of President, or acting as President, during the term within which this Article becomes operative from holding the office of President or acting as President during the remainder of such term.

Section 2. This article shall be inoperative unless it shall have been ratified as an amendment to the Constitution by the legislatures of three-fourths of the several States within seven years from the date of its submission to the States by the Congress.

Amendment XXIII.†

Section 1. The District constituting the seat of Government of the United States shall appoint in such manner as the Congress may direct:

A number of electors of President and Vice President equal to the whole number of Senators and Representatives in Congress to which the District would be entitled if it were a State, but in no event more than the least populous State; they shall be in addition to those appointed by the States, but they shall be considered, for the purposes of the election of President and Vice President, to be electors appointed by a State; and they shall meet in the District and perform such duties as provided by the twelfth article of amendment.

Section 2. The Congress shall have power to enforce this article by appropriate legislation.

*The Twenty-First Amendment was ratified December 5, 1933.

**The Twenty-Second Amendment was ratified February 27, 1951.

† The Twenty-Third Amendment was ratified March 29, 1961.

Amendment XXIV.*

Section 1. The right of citizens of the United States to vote in any primary or other election for President or Vice President, for electors for President or Vice President, or for Senator or Representative in Congress, shall not be denied or abridged by the United States or any State by reason of failure to pay any poll tax or other tax.

Section 2. The Congress shall have power to enforce this article by appropriate legislation.

Amendment XXV.**

Section 1. In case of the removal of the President from office or of his death or resignation, the Vice President shall become President.

Section 2. Whenever there is a vacancy in the office of the Vice President, the President shall nominate a Vice President who shall take office upon confirmation by a majority vote of both Houses of Congress.

Section 3. Whenever the President transmits to the President pro tempore of the Senate and the Speaker of the House of Representatives his written declaration that he is unable to discharge the powers and duties of his office, and until he transmits to them a written declaration to the contrary, such powers and duties shall be discharged by the Vice President as Acting President.

Section 4. Whenever the Vice President and a majority of either the principal officers of the executive departments or of such other body as Congress may by law provide, transmit to the President pro tempore of the Senate and the Speaker of the House of Representatives their written declaration that the President is unable to discharge the powers and duties of his office, the Vice President shall immediately assume the powers and duties of the office as Acting President.

Thereafter, when the President transmits to the President pro tempore of the Senate and the Speaker of the House of Representatives his written declaration that no inability exists, he shall resume the powers and duties of his office unless the Vice President and a majority of either the principal officers of the executive department or of such other body as Congress may by law provide, transmit within four days to the President pro tempore of the Senate and the Speaker of the House of Representatives their written declaration that the President is unable to discharge the powers and duties of his office. Thereupon Congress shall decide the issue, assembling within forty-eight hours for that purpose if not in session. If the Congress, within twenty-one days after receipt of the latter written declaration, or, if Congress is not in session, within twenty-one days after Congress is required to assemble, determines by two-thirds vote of both Houses that the President is unable to discharge the powers and duties of his office, the Vice President shall continue to discharge the same as Acting President; otherwise, the President shall resume the powers and duties of his office.

Amendment XXVI*

Section 1. The right of citizens of the United States, who are eighteen years of age or older, to vote shall not be denied or abridged by the United States or by any State on account of age.

Section 2. The Congress shall have power to enforce this article by appropriate legislation.

Amendment XXVII.*

No law, varying the compensation for the services of the Senators and Representatives, shall take effect, until an election of Representatives shall have intervened.

---

*The Twenty-Fourth Amendment was ratified January 23, 1964.

**The Twenty-Fifth Amendment was ratified February 10, 1967.

*The Twenty-Sixth Amendment was ratified July 1, 1971.

*The Twenty-Seventh Amendment was ratified May 8, 1992.

Selected Bibliography

BOOKS

Abraham, Henry J. *The Judicial Process*. 6th ed. New York: Oxford University Press, 1993.

————. *The Judiciary: The Supreme Court in the Governmental Process*. 8th ed. Dubuque, IA: Wm C. Brown, 1991.

————. *Justices and Presidents: A Political History of Appointments to the Supreme Court*. 3d ed. New York: Oxford University Press, 1992.

Ackerman, Bruce. *We the People: Foundations*. Cambridge, MA: Harvard University Press, Belknap Press, 1991.

Adams, Henry. *The Formative Years: A History of the United States During the Administration of Jefferson and Madison*. Ed. Herbert Agar. 2 vols. London: Collins, 1948.

American Political Science Association and American Historical Association. *This Constitution: Our Enduring Legacy* (Washington, DC: Congressional Quarterly, 1986).

Ames, Herman. *The Proposed Amendments of the Constitution of the United States During the First Century of Its History*. New York: Burt Franklin, 1970; reprint of 1896 edition.

Anastaplo, George. *The Constitution of 1787: A Commentary*. Baltimore, MD: Johns Hopkins University Press, 1989.

Barber, Sotorious A. *On What the Constitution Means*. Baltimore, MD: Johns Hopkins University Press, 1984.

Barnette, Randy E. *The Rights Retained by the People: The History and Meaning of the Ninth Amendment*. Fairfax, VA: George Mason University Press, 1989.

Becker, Theodore J. and Malcolm M. Feeley, eds. *The Impact of Supreme Court Decisions*. 2d ed. New York: Oxford University Press, 1973.

Berger, Raoul. *Government by Judiciary: The Transformation of the Fourteenth Amendment*. Cambridge, MA: Harvard University Press, 1977.

Bernstein, Richard B. with Jerome Agel. *Amending America: If We Love the Constitution So Much, Why Do We Keep Trying To Change It?* New York: Times Books, 1993.

Berry, Mary F. *Why ERA Failed*. Bloomington: Indiana University Press, 1986.

Bickel, Alexander M. *The Least Dangerous Branch: The Supreme Court at the Bar of Politics*. 2d ed. New Haven, CT: Yale University Press, 1986.

————. *The Supreme Court and the Idea of Progress*. New Haven, CT: Yale University Press, 1978.

Black, Hugo. *A Constitutional Faith*. New York: Alfred A. Knopf, 1969.

Boyd, Steven R. *Alternative Constitutions for the United States: A Documentary History*. Westport, CT: Greenwood Press, 1992.

Bryce, James. *Constitutions*. Germany: Scientia Verlag Aalen, 1980; reprint of New York and London, 1905.

Burgess, Susan R. *Contest for Constitutional Authority: The Abortion and War Powers Debates*. Lawrence: University Press of Kansas, 1992.

Burnham, Walter D. *Critical Elections and the Mainsprings of American Politics*. New York: W. W. Norton, 1970.

Burt, Robert A. *The Constitution in Conflict*. Cambridge, MA: Harvard University Press, 1992.

Caplan, Russell L. *Constitutional Brinkmanship: Amending the Constitution by National Convention*. New York: Oxford University Press, 1988.

Cardozo, Benjamin. *The Nature of the Judicial Process*. New Haven, CT: Yale University Press, 1949.

Ceasar, James W. *Liberal Democracy and Political Science*. Baltimore, MD: Johns Hopkins University Press, 1990.

Cortner, Richard C. *The Iron Horse and the Constitution: The Railroads and the Transformation of the Fourteenth Amendment*. Westport, CT: Greenwood Press, 1993.

Craig, Barbara H. and David M. O'Brien. *Abortion and American Politics*. Chatham, NJ: Chatham House Publishers, 1993.

DiClerico, Robert E. *The American President*, 3d ed. Englewood Cliffs, NJ: Prentice-Hall, 1990.

Dworkin, Ronald. *Taking Rights Seriously*. Cambridge, MA: Harvard University Press, 1977.

Ely, John H. *Democracy and Distrust*. Cambridge, MA: Harvard University Press, 1980.

Epstein, Lee and Joseph F. Kobylka. *The Supreme Court and Legal Change: Abortion and the Death Penalty*. Chapel Hill: University of North Carolina Press, 1992.

Ernst, Morris L. *The Great Reversals: Tales of the Supreme Court*. New York: Weybright and Talley, 1973.

Farrand, Max, ed. *The Records of the Federal Convention of 1787*. 4 vols. New Haven, CT: Yale University Press, 1966.

Fisher, Louis. *Constitutional Dialogues: Interpretation as Political Process*. Princeton, NJ: Princeton University Press, 1988.

Fisher, Louis and Neal Devins. *Political Dynamics of Constitutional Law*. St. Paul, MN: West Publishing, 1992.

Foley, Michael. *The Silence of Constitutions: Gaps, Abeyances and Political Temperament in the Maintenance of Government*. London: Routledge, 1989.

Friederich, Carl J. *Constitutional Government and Democracy*. Boston: Ginn and Company, 1946.

Garrow, David J. *Liberty and Sexuality: The Right to Privacy and the Making of Roe v. Wade*. New York: Macmillan, 1994.

Gillman, Howard. *The Constitution Besieged: The Rise and Demise of Lochner Era Police Powers Jurisprudence*. Durham, NC: Duke University Press, 1993.

Glendon, Mary Ann. *Rights Talk: The Impoverishment of Political Discourse*. New York: The Free Press, 1991.

Graham, Howard Jay. *Everyman's Constitution: Historical Essays on the Fourteenth Amendment, the "Conspiracy Theory," and American Constitutionalism*. Madison: State Historical Society of Wisconsin, 1968.

Grimes, Alan P. *Democracy and the Amendments to the Constitution*. Lexington, MA: Lexington Books, 1978.

Hall, Kermit L. *The Oxford Companion to the Supreme Court of the United States*. New York: Oxford University Press, 1992.

Hall, Kermit L., Harold M. Hyman, and Leon V. Sigal. *The Constitutional Convention as an Amending Device*. Washington, DC: The American Historical Association and The American Political Science Association, 1981.

Hamilton, Alexander, James Madison, and John Jay. *The Federalist Papers*, intro by Clinton Rossiter. New York: New American Library, 1961.

Harris, Daryl B. *Proposed Amendments to the U.S. Constitution: 99th–101st Congresses (1985–1990)*. Washington, DC: Congressional Research Service, July 9, 1992.

Harris, William F., II, *The Interpretable Constitution*. Baltimore, MD: Johns Hopkins University Press, 1993.

Hickok, Eugene W. and Gary L. McDowell. *Justice vs. Law: Courts and Politics in American Society*. New York: The Free Press, 1993.

Hofstader, Richard. *The Idea of a Party System: The Rise of Legitimate Opposition in the United States, 1780–1840*. Berkeley: University of California Press, 1972.

Horan, Dennis J., Edward R. Grant, and Paige C. Cunningham, eds. *Abortion and the Constitution: Reversing Roe v. Wade Through the Courts*. Washington, DC: Georgetown University Press, 1987.

Horwill, Herbert W. *The Usages of the American Constitution*. Port Washington, NY: Kennikat Press, 1969.

James, Joseph B. *The Ratification of the Fourteenth Amendment*. Macon, GA: Mercer University Press, 1984.

Kammen, Michael. *A Machine That Would Go of Itself: The Constitution in American Culture*. New York: Alfred A. Knopf, 1987.

Kens, Paul. *Judicial Power and Reform Politics: The Anatomy of Lochner v. New York*. Lawrence: University of Kansas Press, 1990.

Ketcham, Ralph. *Framed for Posterity: The Enduring Philosophy of the Constitution*. Lawrence: University Press of Kansas, 1993.

Keynes, Edward with Randall K. Miller. *The Court vs. Congress: Prayer, Busing, and Abortion*. Durham, NC: Duke University Press, 1989.

Kluger, Richard. *Simple Justice*. 2 vols. New York: Alfred A. Knopf, 1975.

Kuhn, Thomas. *The Structure of Scientific Revolutions*, 2d ed. Chicago: University of Chicago Press, 1970.

Kyvig, David E., ed. *Alcohol and Order: Perspectives on National Prohibition*. Westport, CT: Greenwood Press, 1985.

Lamb, Charles M. and Stephen C. Halpern, eds. *The Burger Court: Political and Judicial Profiles*. Urbana: University of Illinois Press, 1991.

Levy, Leonard, ed. *Encyclopedia of the American Constitution*. 4 vols. New York: Macmillan, 1986.

Lewis, Anthony. *Gideon's Trumpet*. New York: Vintage Books, 1964.

———. *Make No Law: The Sullivan Case and the First Amendment*. New York: Random House, 1991.

Licht, Robert A., ed. *Is the Supreme Court the Guardian of the Constitution?* Washington, DC: AEI Press, 1993.

Lieberman, Jethro K. *The Evolving Constitution*. New York: Random House, 1992.

Lively, Donald E. *Foreshadows of the Law: Supreme Court Dissents and Constitutional Development*. Westport, CT: Praeger, 1992.

Livingston, William S. *Federalism and Constitutional Change*. Oxford: The Clarendon Press, 1956.

Lusky, Louis. *By What Right?* Charlottesville, VA: The Michie Company, 1975.

McNamara, Joseph S. and Lissa Roche. *Still the Law of the Land?* Hillsdale, MI: Hillsdale College Press, 1987.

Malone, Dumas. *Jefferson and the Rights of Man*. Boston: Little, Brown and Company, 1951.

Mansbridge, Jane J. *Why We Lost the ERA*. Chicago: University of Chicago Press, 1986.

Mason, Alpheus T. *The States Rights Debate: Antifederalism and the Constitution*. 2d ed. New York: Oxford University Press, 1972.

———. *The Supreme Court from Taft to Burger*. 3d ed. Baton Rouge: Louisiana State University Press, 1979.

Mason, Alpheus T., and Donald G. Stephenson, Jr. *American Constitutional Law*, 10th ed. Englewood Cliffs, NJ: Prentice-Hall, 1993.

Massaro, John. *Supremely Political: The Role of Ideology and Presidential Management in Unsuccessful Supreme Court Nominations*. Albany: State University of New York Press, 1990.

May, Christopher N. *In the Name of War*. Cambridge, MA: Harvard University Press, 1989.

Mayhew, David R. *Divided We Govern: Party Control, Lawmaking and Investigations, 1946–1990*. New Haven, CT: Yale University Press, 1991.

Mazmanian, Daniel A. and Paul A. Sabatier, eds. *Implementation and Public Policy*. Lexington, MA: Lexington Books, 1991.

Melnick, R. Shep. *Regulation and the Courts: The Case of the Clean Air Act*. Washington, DC: The Brookings Institution, 1983.

Miller, Charles A. *The Supreme Court and the Uses of History*. Cambridge, MA: Harvard University Press, Belknap Press, 1969.

Miller, William L. *The Business of May Next: James Madison and the Founding*. Charlottesville: University Press of Virginia, 1992.

Moore, W. S. and Rudolph G. Penner. *The Constitution and the Budget*. Washington, DC: American Enterprise Institute for Public Policy Research, 1980.

Murphy, Walter F. *Congress and the Court*. Chicago: University of Chicago Press, 1962.

Murphy, Walter F., James E. Fleming, and William F. Harris, eds. *American Constitutional Interpretation*. Mineola, NY: Foundation Press, 1986.

Murphy, Walter F., and C. Herman Pritchett. *Courts, Judges and Politics: An Introduction to the Judicial Process*. 4th ed. New York: Random House, 1986.

Nagel, Robert F. *Constitutional Cultures: The Mentality and Consequences of Judicial Review*. Berkeley: University of California Press, 1989.

Nelson, Michael, ed. *Guide to the Presidency*. Washington, DC: Congressional Quarterly, 1989.

Nelson, William E. *The Fourteenth Amendment: From Political Principle to Judicial Doctrine*. Cambridge, MA: Harvard University Press, 1988.

Neustadt, Richard. *Presidential Power: The Politics of Leadership*. New York: John Wiley and Sons, 1960.

Nisbit, Robert. *History of the Idea of Progress*. New York: Basic Books, 1980.

Orfield, Gary. *Congressional Power: Congress and Social Change*. New York: Harcourt Brace Jovanovich, 1975.

Orfield, Lester B. *The Amending of the Federal Constitution*. Ann Arbor: University of Michigan Press, 1942.

Pennock, Roland and John W. Chapman, eds. *Constitutionalism*. New York: New York University Press, 1979.

Perry, Michael J. *The Constitution, the Courts and Human Rights*. New Haven, CT: Yale University Press, 1982.

Powell, H. Jefferson. *The Moral Tradition of American Constitutionalism: A Theological Interpretation*. Durham, NC: Duke University Press, 1993.

Pressman, Jeffrey I. and Aaron Wildavsky. *Implementation*, 3d. ed. Berkeley: University of California Press, 1984.

Price, Don K. *America's Unwritten Constitution: Science, Religion, and Political Responsibility.* Cambridge, MA: Harvard University Press, 1985.

Rabkin, Jeremy. *Judicial Compulsions: How Public Law Distorts Public Policy.* New York: Basic Books, 1989.

Rakove, Jack N., ed. *Interpreting the Constitution: The Debate Over Original Intent.* Boston: Northeastern University Press, 1990.

Rehnquist, William H. *Grand Inquests: The Historic Impeachments of Justice Samuel Chase and President Andrew Johnson.* New York: William Morrow, 1992.

Richards, David A. J. *Conscience and the Constitution: History, Theory and Law of the Reconstruction Amendments.* Princeton, NJ: Princeton University Press, 1993.

Ripley, Randall B. and Grace A. Franklin. *Congress, the Bureaucracy, and Public Policy.* 5th ed. Pacific Grove, CA: Brooks/Cole Publishing Company, 1991.

Rosenberg, Gerald N. *The Hollow Hope: Can Courts Bring About Social Change?* Chicago: University of Chicago, 1991.

Rossum, Ralph A. and G. Alan Tarr. *American Constitutional Law: Cases and Interpretation.* 3d ed. New York: St. Martin's Press, 1991.

Smith, Christopher E. *Courts and Public Policy.* Chicago: Nelson-Hall, 1993.

Smith, James, ed. *Derecho Constitucional Comparado Mexico-Estados Unidos.* Mexico: Universidad Nacional Autonoma de Mecico, 1990.

Solberg, Winton U. *The Federal Convention and the Formation of the Union of the American States.* New York: Liberal Arts Press, 1958.

Story, Joseph. *Commentaries on the Constitution of the United States.* 3 vols. Boston: Hillard, Gray and Company, 1833.

Suber, Peter. *The Paradox of Self-Amendment.* New York: Peter Lang, 1990.

Sunstein, Cass R. *The Partial Constitution.* Cambridge, MA: Harvard University Press, 1993.

Tananbaum, Duane. *The Bricker Amendment Controversy: A Test of Eisenhower's Political Leadership.* Ithaca, NY: Cornell University Press, 1988.

Tiedeman, Christopher G. *The Unwritten Constitution of the United States.* New York: G. P. Putnam's Sons, 1890.

Tribe, Laurence H. *Abortion: The Clash of Absolutes.* New York: W. W. Norton, 1990.

Urofsky, Melvin I. *A March of Liberty: A Constitutional History of the United States.* New York: Alfred A. Knopf, 1988.

Vile, John R. *A Companion to the United States Constitution and Its Amendments.* Westport, CT: Praeger, 1993.

———. *The Constitutional Amending Process in American Political Thought.* New York: Praeger, 1992.

———. *Contemporary Questions Surrounding the Constitutional Amending Process.* Westport, CT: Praeger, 1993.

———. *Rewriting the United States Constitution: An Examination of Proposals from Reconstruction to the Present.* New York: Praeger, 1991.

———. *The Theory and Practice of Constitutional Change in America: A Collection of Original Source Materials*. New York: Peter Lang, 1993.

Vile, M.J.C. *Constitutionalism and the Separation of Powers*. Oxford: Clarendon Press, 1967.

Vose, Clement. *Constitutional Change: Amendment Politics and Supreme Court Litigation Since 1900*. Lexington, MA: Lexington Books, 1972.

Walker, David M. *The Oxford Companion to Law*. Oxford: Clarendon Press, 1980.

Weber, Paul J. and Barbara Perry. *Unfounded Fears: Myths and Realities of a Constitutional Convention*. New York: Praeger, 1989.

Wills, Garry. *Inventing America: Jefferson's Declaration of Independence*. Garden City, NY: Doubleday, 1978.

Wilson, James Q. *American Government: Brief Version*. 2d ed. Lexington, MA: D. C. Heath, 1990.

Wilson, Woodrow. *Constitutional Government in the United States*. New York: Columbia University Press, 1961; reprint of 1908 edition.

Wood, Stephen B. *Constitutional Politics in the Progressive Era: Child Labor and the Law*. Chicago: University of Chicago Press, 1968.

ARTICLES AND ESSAYS

Ackerman, Bruce. "The Storrs Lectures: Discovering the Constitution." *The Yale Law Journal* 93 (May 1984), 1013–72.

———. "Transformative Appointments." *Harvard Law Review* 101 (1988), 1164–84.

Amar, Akil R. "The Bill of Rights as a Constitution." *Yale Law Journal* 100 (Winter 1992), 1131–1210.

———. "Philadelphia Revisited: Amending the Constitution Outside Article V." *University of Chicago Law Review* 55 (Fall 1988), 1043–1104.

Aynes, Richard L. "On Misreading John Bingham and the Fourteenth Amendment." *The Yale Law Review* 103 (October 1993), 57–104.

"The Balanced Budget Amendment: An Inquiry Into Appropriateness." *Harvard Law Review* 96 (May 1983), 1600–20.

Bernstein, Richard B. "Fixing the Electoral College." *Constitution* 5 (Winter 1993), 42–50.

———. "The Sleeper Wakes: The History and Legacy of the Twenty-Seventh Amendment." *Fordham Law Review* 61 (December 1992), 497–557.

Berry, Mary F. "How Hard It Is To Change." *New York Times Magazine* (September 23, 1987), 93–98.

Boudreaux, Donald J. and A. C. Pritchard. "Rewriting the Constitution: An Economic Analysis of the Constitutional Amendment Process." *Fordham Law Review* 62 (October 1993), 111–62.

Brennan, Thomas E. "Return to Philadelphia." *Cooley Law Review* 1 (1982), 1–82.

Brennan, William J., Jr. "The Constitution of the United States: Contemporary Ratification." *South Texas Law Review* 27 (Fall 1986), 433–45.

———. "State Constitutions and the Protection of Individual Rights." *Harvard Law Review* 90 (January 1977), 489–504.

Brown, Everett S. "The Ratification of the Twenty-First Amendment." *The American Political Science Review* 29 (December 1935), 1005–17.

Brown, Jennifer K. "The Nineteenth Amendment and Women's Equality." *The Yale Law Journal* 102 (June 1993), 2174–2204.

"The Civil Rights Act of 1991 and Less Discriminatory Alternatives in Disparate Impact Litigation." *Harvard Law Review* 106 (May 1993), 1621–38.

Clymer, Adam. "Abortion Rights Bill Gives Way to Other Priorities in Congress." *The New York Times* (September 16, 1993), A1, A11.

"Congressional Reversal of Supreme Court Decisions: 1945–1956." *Harvard Law Review* 71 (1958), 1324–37.

Davidson, Roger H. "The Lawmaking Congress." *Law and Contemporary Problems* 56 (Autumn 1993), 99–120.

Davis, Sue. "Constitutional Change Through Judicial Review: A Dialectical View." Paper prepared for presentation at the annual meeting of the Southwestern Social Science Association, San Antonio, Texas, March 1986.

Dellinger, Walter. "The Amending Process in Canada and the United States: A Contemporary Perspective." *Law and Contemporary Problems* 45 (Autumn 1982), 283–302.

———. "The Legitimacy of Constitutional Change: Rethinking the Amending Process." *Harvard Law Review* 97 (1983), 380–432.

Devins, Neal S. "Correspondence: The Stuff of Constitutional Law." *Iowa Law Review* 77 (July 1992), 1795–1801.

Donovan, Beth. "Clinton Reverses Directives; Battle Begins Anew." *Congressional Quarterly Weekly* 51 (January 23, 1993), 182.

Eiselen, Malcolm R. "Dare We Call a Federal Convention?" *The North American Review* 244 (Autumn 1937), 26–38.

Eskridge, William N., Jr. "Overriding Supreme Court Statutory Interpretation Decisions." *The Yale Law Journal* 101 (November 1991), 331–455.

Freund, Paul A. "To Amend—or Not to Amend the Constitution." *New York Times Magazine* (December 13, 1964), 33, 117–20.

Gerhardt, Michael J. "The Role of Precedent in Constitutional Decisionmaking and Theory." *The George Washington Law Review* 60 (November 1991), 68–159.

Ginsberg, Ruth B. "On Amending the Constitution: A Plea for Patience." *University of Arkansas at Little Rock Law Journal* 12 (1989–90), 677–94.

Goldstein, Leslie F. "The ERA and the U.S. Supreme Court." *Research in Law and Policy Studies*, vol. 1, ed. Stuart S. Nagel. Greenwich, CT: JAI Press, 1987, 145–61.

Grey, Thomas C. "Do We Have an Unwritten Constitution?" *Stanford Law Review* 27 (February 1975), 703–18.

Hamburger, Philip A. "The Constitution's Accommodation of Social Change." *Michigan Law Review* 88 (November 1989), 238–327.

Henschen, Beth M. and Edward I. Sidlow. "The Supreme Court and the Congressional Agenda-Setting Process." *The Journal of Law & Politics* 5 (1989), 685–724.

Herrmann, Mark E. "Looking Down from the Hill: Factors Determining the Success of Congressional Efforts to Reverse Supreme Court Interpretations of the Constitution." *William and Mary Law Review* 33 (Winter 1992), 543–610.

Horn, Dottie. "Another Star for the Stripes?" *Endeavors* 8 (Fall 1990), 4–6.

Kay, Richard S. "The Illegality of the Constitution." *Constitutional Commentary* 4 (Winter 1987), 57–80.

Kennedy, Christopher M. "Is There a Twenty-Seventh Amendment? The Unconstitutionality of a 'New' 203-Year-Old Amendment." *The John Marshall Law Review* 26 (September 1993), 977–1019.

Keogh, Stephen. "Formal and Informal Constitutional Lawmaking in the United States in the Winter of 1860–1861." *Journal of Legal History* 8 (December 1987), 275–99.

Klarman, Michael J. "*Brown*, Racial Change, and the Civil Rights Movement." *Virginia Law Review* 80 (February 1994), 7–150.

Kozinski, Alex and Eugene Volokh. "A Penumbra Too Far." *Harvard Law Review* 106 (May 1993), 1639–57.

Kyvig, David E. "The Road Not Taken: FDR, the Supreme Court, and Constitutional Amendment." *Political Science Quarterly* 104 (Fall 1989), 463–81.

Lee, R. Alton. "The Corwin Amendment in the Secession Crisis." *Ohio Historical Quarterly* 70 (January 1961), 1–26.

Leuchenburg, William E. "The Origins of Franklin D. Roosevelt's 'Court-Packing' Plan." *Supreme Court Review*, ed. Philip Kurland. Chicago: University of Chicago Press, 1966, 347–400.

Levinson, Sanford. "Accounting for Constitutional Change (Or, How Many Times Has the United States Constitution Been Amended? (A) < 26; (B) 26; (C) > 26; (D) All of the Above)." *Constitutional Commentary* 8 (Summer 1991), 409–31.

———. "On the Constitution's Text: The Problem of the (So-Called) Twenty-Seventh Amendment." Forthcoming in *Constitutional Commentary*.

———. "On the Notion of Amendment: Reflections on David Daube's Jehovah the Good." *S'Vara: A Journal of Philosophy and Judaism* 1 (Winter 1990), 25–31.

Lipkin, Robert J. "The Anatomy of Constitutional Revolutions." *Nebraska Law Review* 68 (1989), 701–806.

Lupu, Ira C. "Statutes Revolving in Constitutional Law Orbits." *Virginia Law Review* 79 (February 1992), 1–89.

Lutz, Donald S. "Toward a Theory of Constitutional Amendment." Paper presented at the American Political Science Association in Chicago, Illinois, September, 1992.

McDowell, Gary L. "On Meddling with the Constitution." *Journal of Contemporary Studies* 5 (Fall 1982), 3–17.

McGovney, D. O. "Is the Eighteenth Amendment Void Because of Its Contents?" *Columbia Law Review* 20 (May 1920), 499–518.

Markman, Stephen J. "The Amendment Process of Article V: A Microcosm of the Constitution." *Harvard Journal of Law & Public Policy*, 12 (1989), 113–21.

Marshall, Thomas R. "Policymaking and the Modern Court: When Do Supreme Court Rulings Prevail?" *Western Political Quarterly* 42 (December 1989), 493–507.

Masci, David. "Religious Freedom Bill Wins Subcommittee Approval." *Congressional Quarterly Weekly* 51 (March 20, 1993), 676.

Mendleson, Wallace. "Sex and the Singular Constitution: What Remains of *Roe v. Wade?*" *PS: Political Science & Politics*, 26 (June 1993), 206–8.

Miller, Arthur S. "Lord Chancellor, Warren Earl Burger." *Society* 10 (March/April 1973), 18–27.

Miller, Geoffrey P. "The President's Power of Interpretation: Implications of a Unified Theory of Constitutional Law." *Law and Contemporary Problems* 56 (Autumn 1993), 35–62.

Mills, Mike. "Cost of Senate NIH Approval Is Continued Immigrant Ban." *Congressional Quarterly Weekly* 51 (February 20, 1993), 391.

Munzer, Stephen R. and James W. Nickel. "Does the Constitution Mean What It Always Meant?" *Columbia Law Review* 77 (November 1977), 1029–62.

Murphy, Walter. "An Ordering of Constitutional Values." *Southern California Law Review* 53 (January 1980), 703–60.

Myers, Denys P. *The Process of Constitutional Amendment.* Senate Document No. 314, 76th Congress, 3d Session, 1940.

Nagel, Stuart S. "Court-Curbing Proposals in American History." *Vanderbilt Law Review* 18 (1965), 925–44.

Paulsen, Michael S. "A General Theory of Article V: The Constitutional Lessons of the Twenty-Seventh Amendment." *The Yale Law Journal* 103 (December 1993), 677–789.

Pedrick, William H. and Richard C. Dahl. "Let the People Vote! Ratification of Constitutional Amendments by Convention." *Arizona Law Review* 30 (1988), 243–56.

Peebles, Thomas H. "A Call to High Debate: The Organic Constitution in Its Formative Era, 1890–1920." *University of Colorado Law Review* 52 (Fall 1980), 49–104.

Pope, James G. "Republican Moments: The Role of Direct Popular Power in the American Constitutional Order." *University of Pennsylvania Law Review* 139 (December 1990), 287–368.

Powell, H. Jefferson. "The Political Grammar of Early Constitutional Law." *North Carolina Law Review* 71 (April 1993), 949–1009.

Radin, Max. "The Intermittent Sovereign." *Yale Law Journal* 39 (1930), 514–31.

"Religious Freedom Bill OK'd." *The Christian Century* 110 (November 10, 1993), 1116–17.

Richards, David A. J. "Revolution and Constitutionalism in America." *Cardozo Law Review* 14 (January 1993), 577–634.

Rosenberg, Gerald N. "*Brown* is Dead! Long Live *Brown*!: The Endless Attempt to Canonize a Case." *Virginia Law Review* 80 (February 1994), 161–72.

Rubin, Alissa J. "Freedom of Choice Bill Returns; Too Early to Predict Outcome." *Congressional Quarterly Weekly* 51 (March 20, 1993), 675.

Rubin, Alissa J., with Jill Zuchman. "Abortion Funding Rebuff Shows House Divided." *Congressional Quarterly Weekly* 51 (July 3, 1993), 1735–39.

Sargentich, Thomas O. "The Limits of the Parliamentary Critique of the Separation of Powers." *William and Mary Law Review* 34 (Spring 1993), 679–739.

Schwarz, Frederick A. O., Jr. "The Constitution Outside the Courts." *Cardozo Law Review* 14 (April 1993), 1287–310.

Sherry, Suzanna. "The Founders' Unwritten Constitution." *The University of Chicago Law Review* 54 (1987), 1127–77.

Stone, Geoffrey R. "In Opposition to the School Prayer Amendment." *The University of Chicago Law Review* 50 (Spring 1983), 823–48.

———. "Precedent, the Amendment Process, and Evolution in Constitutional Doctrine." *Harvard Journal of Law & Public Policy* 11 (Winter 1988), 67–73.

Strickland, Ruth A. "Population Size, Diversity and the Proclivity of States to Oppose or Support the Ratification of Amendments to the U.S. Constitution." *Southeastern Political Review* 20 (Fall 1992), 269–93.

———. "The Twenty-Seventh Amendment and Constitutional Change by Stealth." *PS: Political Science & Politics* 26 (December 1993), 716–22.

Suber, Peter. "Population Changes and Constitutional Amendments: Federalism versus Democracy." *Journal of Law Reform* 20 (Winter 1987), 409–90.

Tribe, Laurence. "Issues Raised by Requesting Congress to Call a Constitutional Convention to Propose a Balanced Budget Amendment." *Pacific Law Journal* 10 (1979), 627–39.

Turner, John J., Jr. "The Twelfth Amendment and the First American Party System." *The Historian* 35 (1973), 221–37.

Van Alstyne, William. "Notes on a Bicentennial Constitution: Part I, Processes of Change." *University of Illinois Law Review* (1984), 933–58.

———. "What Do You Think About the Twenty-Seventh Amendment?" *Constitutional Commentary* 10 (Winter 1993), 9–18.

Vile, John R. "Just Say No to 'Stealth' Amendment." *The National Law Journal* 14 (June 22, 1992), 15–16.

———. "Proposals to Amend the Bill of Rights: Are Fundamental Rights in Jeopardy?" *Judicature* 75 (August–September 1991), 62–67.

———. "Three Kinds of Constitutional Founding and Change: The Convention Model and Its Alternatives." *Political Research Quarterly* (December 1993), 881–95.

Vose, Clement. "When District of Columbia Representation Collides with the Constitutional Amending Institution." *Publius: The Journal of Federalism* 9 (Winter 1979), 105–25.

Williams, George W. "What If Any, Limitations Are There Upon the Power To Amend the Constitution of the United States?" *Virginia Law Register* n.s. 6 (July 1920), 161–74.

Table of Cases

Index

About the Author

JOHN R. VILE is Professor and Chair in the Department of Political Science at Middle Tennessee State University. He is the author of *Rewriting the United States Constitution* (Praeger, 1991), *The Constitutional Amending Process in American Political Thought* (Praeger, 1992), *A Companion to the United States Constitution and Its Amendments* (Praeger, 1993), and *Contemporary Questions Surrounding the Constitutional Amending Process* (Praeger, 1993), and is the editor of *The Theory and Practice of Constitutional Change in America* (1993).

ISBN 0-275-94918-4

90000>

EAN

9 780275 949181

HARDCOVER BAR CODE